Little
BIG STUFF

PINT-SIZED PLAY SETS TO SEW FOR KIDS

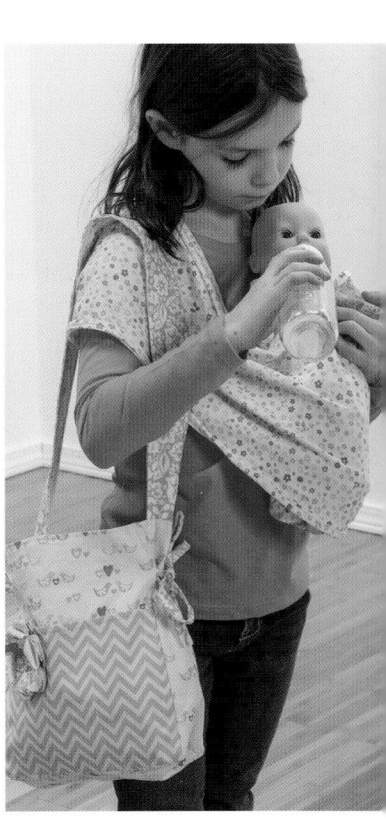

MICHELLE LEE JENSEN

Martingale
Create with Confidence

Dedication

For my dad, my first pattern editor. We have come a long way, and now have a whole amazing team to share my dreams. I love you and miss you.

For my husband and children. Thank you for putting up with late nights, early mornings, and sometimes too much sewing. I love you all an immeasurable amount.

Little Big Stuff: Pint-Sized Play Sets to Sew for Kids
© 2015 by Michelle Lee Jensen

Martingale®
19021 120th Ave. NE, Ste. 102
Bothell, WA 98011-9511 USA
ShopMartingale.com

Printed in China
20 19 18 17 16 15   8 7 6 5 4 3 2 1

Library of Congress Cataloging-in-Publication Data
is available upon request.

ISBN: 978-1-60468-530-5

MISSION STATEMENT

Dedicated to providing quality products and service to inspire creativity.

CREDITS

PUBLISHER AND CHIEF VISIONARY OFFICER
Jennifer Erbe Keltner

EDITORIAL DIRECTOR
Karen Costello Soltys

DESIGN DIRECTOR
Paula Schlosser

ACQUISITIONS EDITOR
Karen M. Burns

PHOTOGRAPHER
Brent Kane

TECHNICAL EDITOR
Rebecca Kemp Brent

PRODUCTION MANAGER
Regina Girard

COPY EDITOR
Melissa Bryan

COVER AND
INTERIOR DESIGNER
Adrienne Smitke

ILLUSTRATOR
Christine Erikson

CONTENTS

Introduction   5
Special Touches   7
Useful Techniques   10

Projects

GARDEN GOODNESS   17
Gardening Apron   18
Gardening Bucket   23
Picnic Blanket   26
Picnic Tote   27

SHOP'S OPEN   30
Task Apron   31
Task Basket   34
Play Shop   38

CAMPOUT FUN   40
Sleeping Bag   41
Pillow   43
Duffel Bag   44
Bindle   50
Tent   51

KITCHEN COOKING   54
Tasty Kitchen Apron   55
Tablecloth   58
Oven Mitt and Hot Pads   59

BABY LOVE   62
Diaper Bag and Changing Pad   63
Receiving Blanket, Burp Cloth, and Sling   68

PET PRACTICE   70
Critter Carrier   71
Leash   75
Cozy Bed   76

Acknowledgments   79
About the Author   80

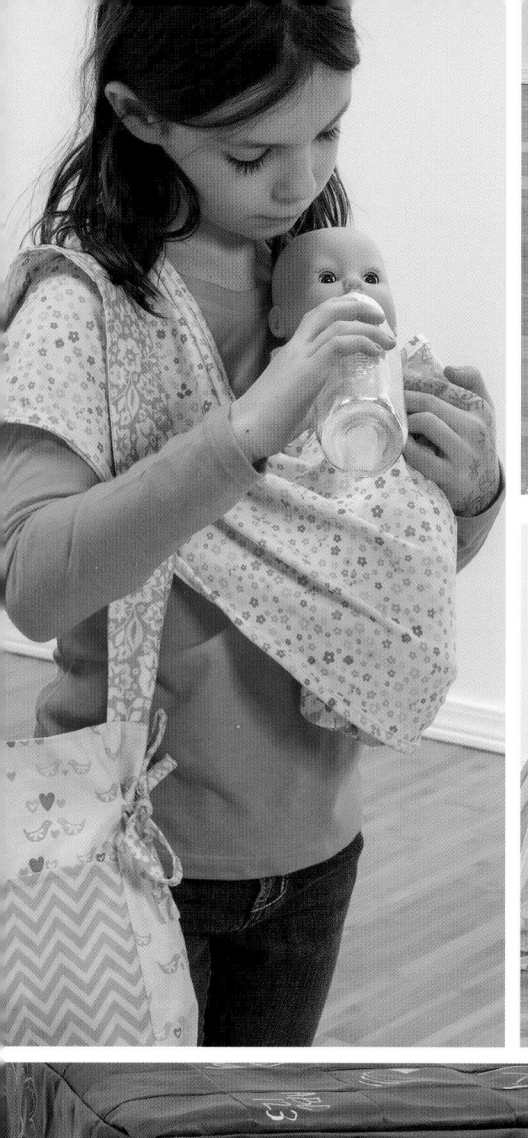

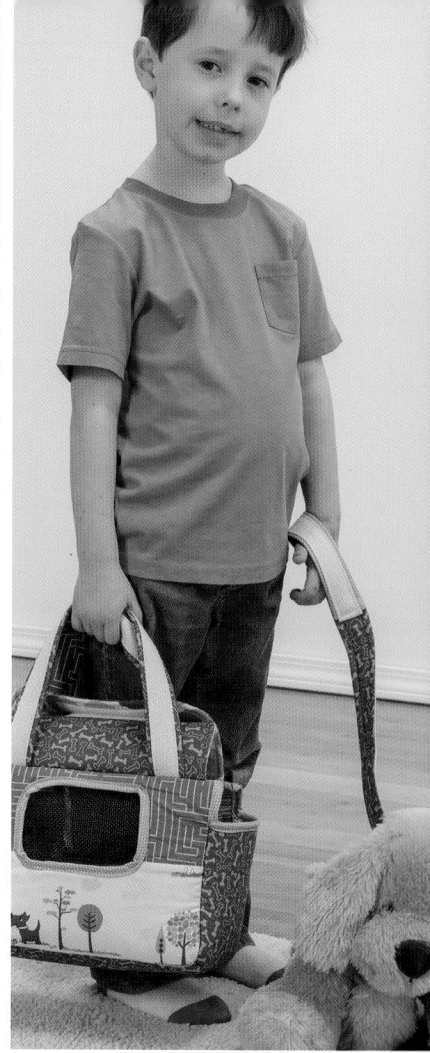

INTRODUCTION

Sewing for children has been such a gratifying experience for me! The first pattern I created was a classic doll's diaper bag, included in this book. I found a passion for creating these items for my children, and that passion has grown immensely because I'm having so much fun.

I could go on and on about the freedom I feel when embarking on the journey of making a bag or apron or carrier for a little sweetheart. I love to begin by learning the child's favorite color, and then I go from there. Working with my scraps and a few carefully selected purchases, it's fun to combine the cute fabrics into palettes I never would have used otherwise. More information about this topic is included in the "Special Touches" section. I hope this same sense of possibility and wonder will help you as you journey through the projects in this book.

You'll find the projects grouped into themed collections that make unforgettable gifts when given together. However, each item is also great on its own. Many projects can even be made for adults—the picnic blanket, for example. A home-sewn item is a rare and cherished article for most people. Receiving this type of gift is heartwarming because of the love, time, and care involved in creating handmade things. I hope you enjoy making these items, and I hope the lucky individuals—big or small—who receive the fruits of your labors are inspired to play boundlessly!

I'm a long-arm quilter and a quilt-pattern designer, but I've discovered that my children really love the more dimensional items I have made. They've tied them around their waists, carried them through their days and the worlds they create for themselves, placed treasured items inside, and found *new uses* I hadn't even considered. Children have wondrous imaginations that are all too easily lost when we grow up. I challenge you to use your imagination just for a while when working with this book. If you have a child who loves art, redefine the gardening collection as art accessories: the apron would work well as a cover-up during arts-and-crafts time, and the gardening bucket would make a great organizer for markers and pencils. If you have a child who loves learning about astronomy, spread the picnic blanket out on the grass for a night of stargazing. Any of the ideas in these pages can be tailored to make a gift that's as unique as the child who will receive it. As if you didn't have enough exciting reasons to get started, I hope I've just given you a few more. Let's get sewing!

~ Michelle

SPECIAL TOUCHES

Adult and juvenile prints combine effectively in this diaper-bag set.

One of the qualities that sets a handmade item apart from a store-bought gift is the opportunity to tailor it—its fabrics and embellishments—for a specific recipient. Here are some ideas to keep in mind.

CHOOSING FABRICS

What I find exciting when making items for children is that the combinations of fabric colors and prints are endless. I'm able to mix more-sophisticated prints with juvenile motifs to achieve something unexpected and fun. A green floral might be thought of as a sophisticated adult fabric, but when paired with a sweet bird print in a pattern for a doll's diaper bag, it becomes part of a distinct combination that works!

Many fabric manufacturers have taken the guesswork out of this process by using a similar formula for combining prints in their fabric collections. However, if you're making some of these children's toys with fabric you have on hand, use my suggestions when building your fabric combinations to increase your choices and create something visually fresh and exciting.

Fabric selection is important when considering different genders for each item as well. For example, the pet carrier can be made entirely in neutral fabrics; however, if you would like to make it specifically for a girl whose favorite color is pink, you can pair a dog-bone print with a pink damask fabric. It is also fun to bring in a variety of different fabrics for pockets, handles, flaps, and so on, that coordinate with the main fabric. These fabrics are a great place to use what you have available, and they add an extra boost of visual interest, too.

Specialty fabrics are especially wonderful to explore. Some projects include fabric you may not have experimented with, such as laminated cotton. Its durability makes it one of my favorite materials to use for children's items.

Make It Your Own

My philosophy is that each sewist should choose the colors and fabrics she likes best. For clarity, the instructions in this book include descriptions of the fabrics used in the photographed projects. However, I hope you'll feel free to choose different color schemes, and even combine several pieces in place of one fabric or subdivide pieces among different fabrics. Consider these instructions your starting point as you create your unique project.

Unless a different fabric is specified, the projects in this book are made from quilter's cottons, 100% cotton woven fabrics. When specialty fabrics such as laminated cotton or canvas are recommended, they're specified in the materials list for the project.

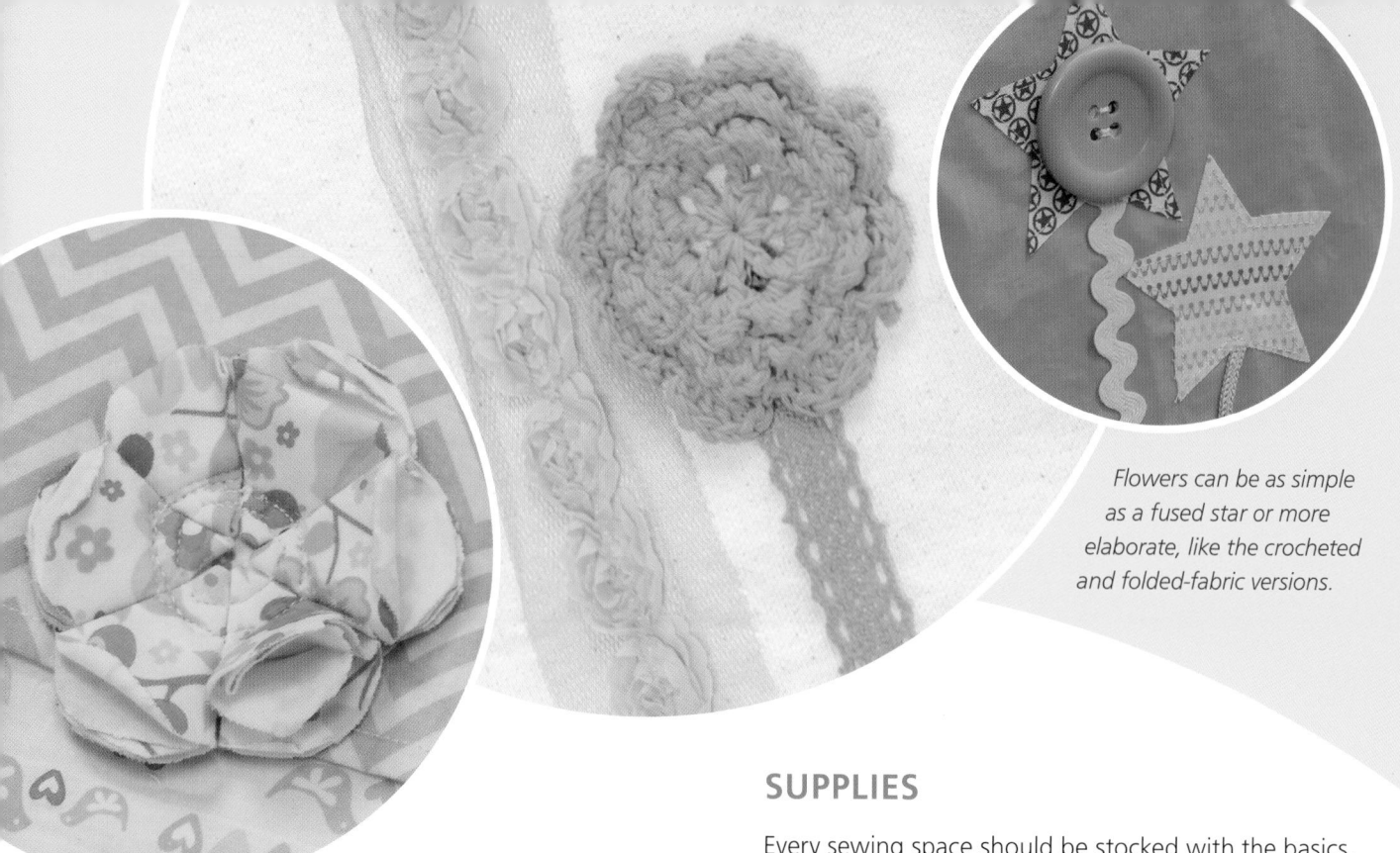

Flowers can be as simple as a fused star or more elaborate, like the crocheted and folded-fabric versions.

ADDING EMBELLISHMENTS

There's really no better way of adding interest to these projects than by using embellishments. They really spice things up! Start simple, such as adding a flower-shaped button to a bag, and then as you get more comfortable branch out into creating a flower embellishment from scratch (see "Making the Flower" on page 66). You can also find beautiful trims to add the special touch that makes a project an heirloom.

Embellishments give every project an additional dimension. They also enhance the feeling that time, care, and personalization were a part of the creative process. I've found that my projects for children have the most impact when I dress up simple, unfussy patterns with beautiful, thoughtfully chosen and constructed embellishments. In this book the projects are in their most simple state, but don't let that stop you from adding embellishments on your own.

The key to embellishment: Don't be afraid! Try new things. Challenge yourself. You'll be amazed and very satisfied with the results!

SUPPLIES

Every sewing space should be stocked with the basics. You'll find the supplies listed below extremely helpful as you make the projects in this book.

Rotary Cutter, Rulers, and Mat

Using these items is the easiest way to cut fabric accurately. Almost all of the pieces are squares, strips, and rectangles, making them perfect for rotary cutting.

Clips

Some of the projects are so thick that pins are difficult to use, and pins will leave holes in laminated fabric. I prefer clips for ease of positioning, sewing, and holding pieces together. They make the process go a little faster. I recommend Wonder Clips from Clover; they are excellent for this purpose.

Notions

Webbing, fusible fleece, interfacing, cord, and trim: all of these items have specific purposes in a project. They're all commonly available at your local fabric shop. Make a list before you head out to gather supplies, and you should have no problem finding everything you need.

MAKE IT YOUR OWN!

Just because I showed the bake set (page 54) in pink for a little girl doesn't mean you have to follow suit. Try a fun polka-dot bake set for a young man in your life. (Boys like making cookies too!)

Turn the shop (page 30) into a salon or fabric store with a colorful floral or geometric print curtain. Choose your child's favorite color to sew a pet bed (page 76), diaper bag (page 63), or any of the other projects in this book. Girls don't all like pink, and blue isn't just for boys. But you knew that, right?!

If the play set you're making isn't a surprise, consider taking your little ones along to the fabric store and let them pick the colors and prints they like best to truly make a gift they will love—and play with—for years to come.

Dress the diaper bag up or down by adding a cute ruffle or using a denim-look fabric.

USEFUL TECHNIQUES

In addition to sewing seams, you'll be using a few other simple techniques for most of the projects in this book. Refer to this section as needed when installing a zipper, adding piping, or attaching binding.

BINDING

Fabric binding makes a great edging for many types of projects including aprons, bags, and blankets, and for creating ties for bags. The greatest thing about binding is its versatility. Binding can be cut on the bias or along the straight of grain of the fabric, but you will need bias-cut binding for many projects in this book to provide stretch that will accommodate curved edges. If the edge to be bound is straight, binding cut on the straight of grain will suffice.

Single-Fold Binding

I used single-fold binding in almost all of the projects in this book. It's very versatile for finishing the edges of three-dimensional items. You'll need 1½"- to 2"-wide strips, depending on the finished binding width of your project; the cut size is approximately four times the finished width. Cut your fabric along the true bias, on a 45° angle from the selvage, unless the project instructions specify straight-grain binding.

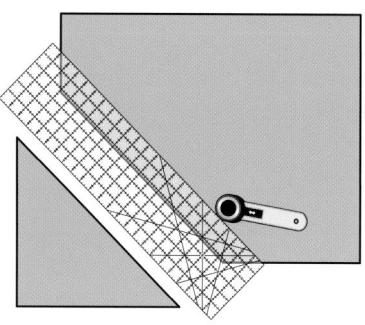

1 Join the cut strips with diagonal seams. Place two strips at right angles to each other, right sides together. Sew across the ends, using a ¼" seam allowance. Press the seam allowances open. Repeat until all the strips are joined into a continuous length.

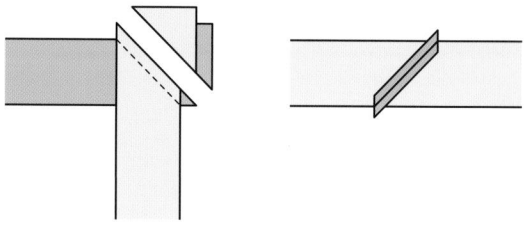

2 Fold the strip in half lengthwise with wrong sides together and press. Open the binding and fold the long raw edges inward to meet at the fold. Press again. Refold along the original crease, encasing the raw edges, and press once more.

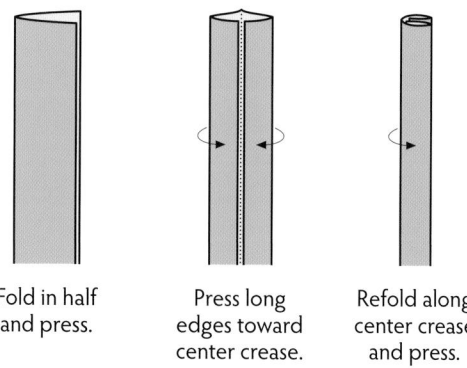

Fold in half and press.   Press long edges toward center crease.   Refold along center crease and press.

3 Insert the raw edge of the project between the binding folds. Leaving a 4" tail free at the beginning of the binding, topstitch ⅛" from the inner edge. Be sure the stitches catch the folds on the front and back surfaces of the project piece.

4 Work your way around the project edge. As you approach the starting point, overlap the ends of the binding 1½" to 2", to match the cut width of the binding strips, and mark. Trim the excess fabric. Unfold the binding ends and rotate them to meet at a right angle, right sides together; pin. Sew across the square where the strips overlap from corner to corner to create a diagonal seam. Trim the seam allowances to ¼". Press the seam allowances open and refold the binding strip. Sew the joined binding to the remaining project edge.

5 If your binding needs to fold around a corner, you'll have to create a miter at the corner to keep the binding smooth. Stop sewing ¼" before reaching the project edge and backstitch. Fold the binding strip around the corner, forming a little mountain of fabric on the front and back surfaces of the binding. Tuck the fold of binding under the straight binding, creating folds at a 45° angle to the project edges. Start sewing again at the corner fold and continue along the next edge of the project.

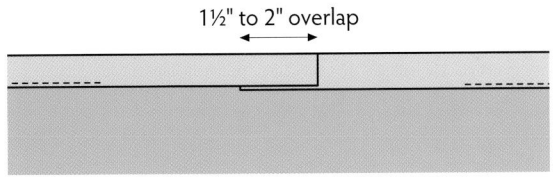

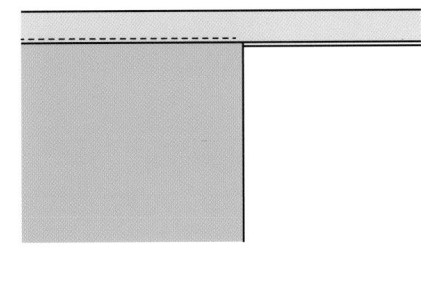

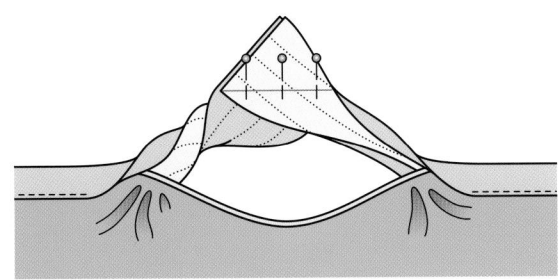

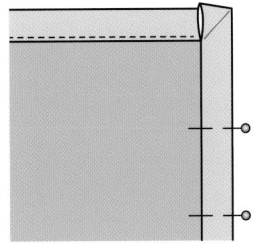
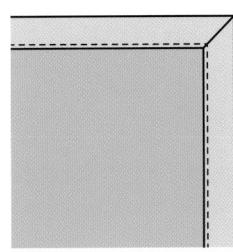

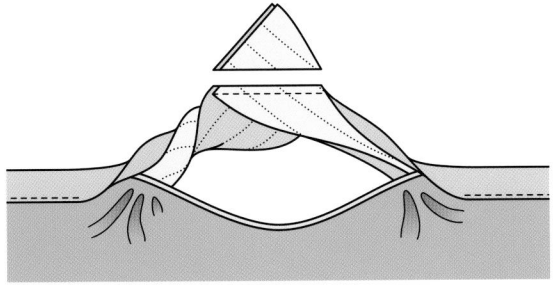

Double-Fold Binding

Double-fold binding is sewn to a project a little differently than single-fold binding. You'll need to begin with 2¼"- to 2½"-wide strips. I prefer the look of the narrower binding, but the wider binding works very well, isn't as tightly wrapped around the project edges, and may be essential for a bulky project. Cut the fabric strips on the true bias, at a 45° angle from the selvage.

1 Cut and join the strips as for single-fold binding on page 10. Fold the strips in half lengthwise with wrong sides together and press.

2 Position the prepared binding on the right side of the project, matching the project and binding raw edges. Leaving a 7" tail free at the beginning, sew the binding to the project with a ¼" seam allowance.

3 Stop sewing ¼" before reaching the project edge. To miter the binding at the corner, fold the binding up and away from the project, forming a fold at a 45° angle to the project edges. Fold the binding back down along the next project edge. Resume sewing at the corner. Continue sewing around all sides of the project until you approach the beginning of the binding.

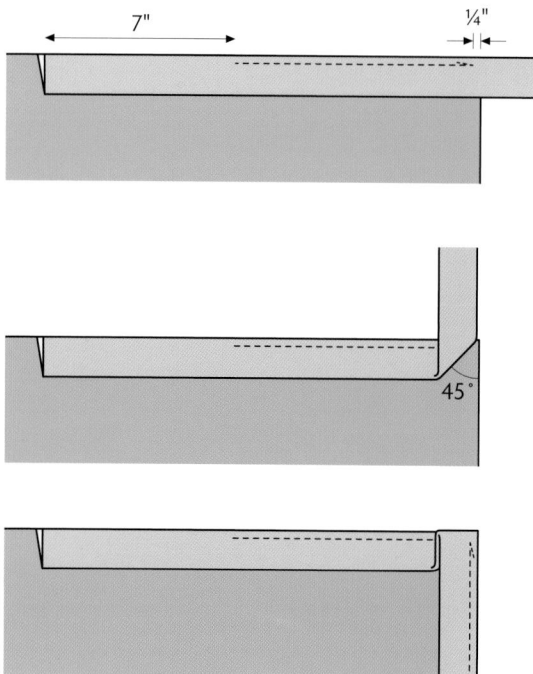

4 Overlap the ends of the binding 2¼" to 2½", to match the cut width of the binding strips, and mark. Trim the excess fabric. Unfold the binding ends and rotate them to meet at a right angle, right sides together; pin. Sew from corner to corner across the square where the strips overlap to create a diagonal seam. Trim the seam allowances to ¼". Press the seam allowances open and refold the binding strip.

2¼" to 2½" overlap

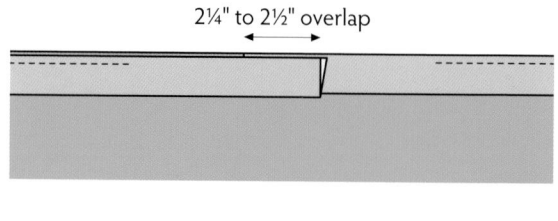

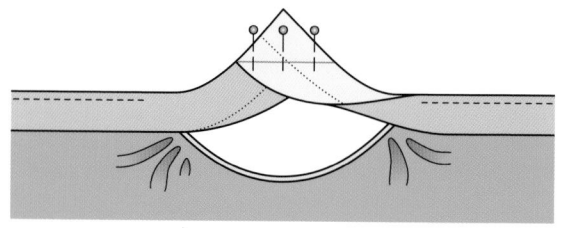

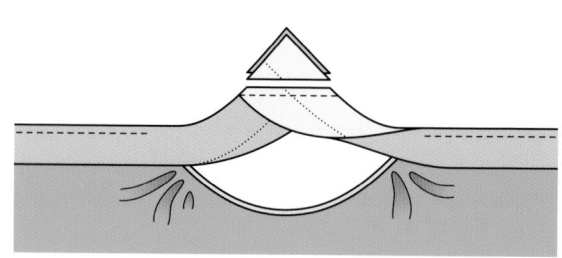

5 Sew the joined binding strip to the remainder of the project edge.

6 Fold the binding over the project raw edge from front to back. Tuck in the corners to complete the miters on the back of the project. The folded edge of the binding should extend 1/16" to 1/8" past the seamline on the back of the project, covering the stitches. Stitch in the ditch (directly on top of the seam) from the front of the project, catching the folded edge on the project back, or edgestitch 1/16" to 1/8" from the fold if working from the back.

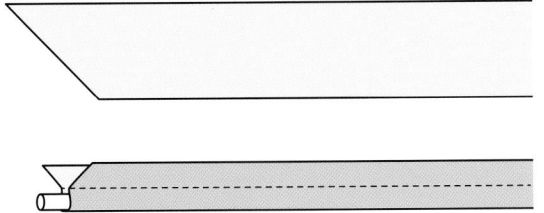
Piping at the pocket edge and along the seam adds a more finished look to your project.

TOPSTITCHED FRENCH SEAMS

A traditional French seam encases the raw fabric edges inside the seam allowances, creating a clean finish both inside and outside. My technique is a slight variation, with the seam allowances left on the outside of the project as a design detail. I've used this technique with a few of the projects in this book.

1 Place the fabrics to be joined with right sides together. Sew, using a scant ¼" seam allowance. You may find it helpful to trim this seam allowance to ⅛" to be sure no raw edges are visible in the finished seam.

2 Press the fabrics open and the seam allowances to one side. Fold the fabrics along the seam with wrong sides together. Sew with a ¼" seam allowance, enclosing the raw edges from the previous seam.

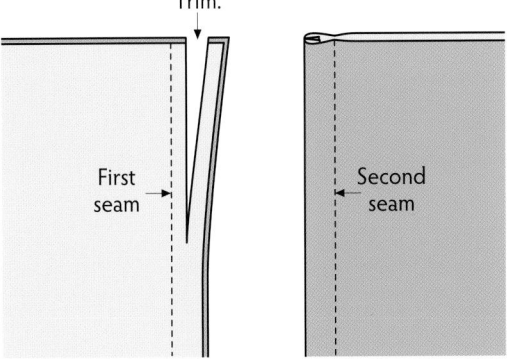

3 Press the completed seam allowances, which will be on the *outside* of the project, to one side. Edgestitch along the loose edge of the seam allowances, securing them to the project.

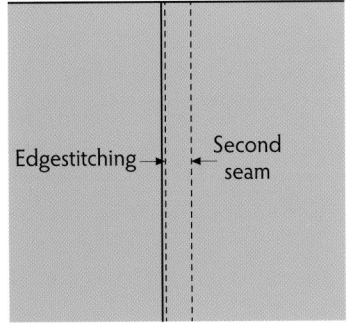

PIPING

Piping (covered cording) is a fun element to add to a bag. It helps define the bag's structure, plus it's quite easy to prepare.

1 Cut bias fabric strips 1½" wide as directed in the project instructions. Join the ends to make a continuous length.

2 Place a length of ¼"-diameter cotton cord along the center of the fabric strip. Fold the fabric lengthwise, wrong sides together, to enclose the cord.

3 Using a zipper foot, sew close to the cord along the entire length of the piping. That's it! Your piping is ready to insert in a seam along the edge of a project.

ZIPPER INSTALLATION

Adding a zipper needn't be complicated. I like creating a zipper panel first and then adding it to my project; working flat makes the zipper installation a piece of cake. Follow along to create your panel.

1 Gather four same-sized fabric pieces, two for the outer layer and two for the lining, and a zipper. The fabric pieces will be longer than the zipper length for this installation technique. Cut two additional fabric rectangles, 2" x 4", for the zipper tabs. Fold each tab rectangle in half crosswise, creating a 2" x 2" square, and topstitch ¼" from the folded edges.

2 Pin the folded edge of a zipper tab to each end of the zipper. If the zipper is exactly the right length, position the tabs next to the zipper stops at the top and bottom of the zipper. If you'll be shortening the zipper to fit the project, place one tab next to the upper zipper stops—next to the zipper pull when the zipper is closed—and then measure along the zipper to find the correct position for the second tab. Topstitch the tab to the zipper, stitching over the previous topstitching. Sew slowly and carefully across the zipper, and be sure to avoid the metal stops and zipper pull as you stitch. Zipper tabs make sewing across the zipper easier by keeping the zipper ends away from the seams lying perpendicular to the zipper.

3 Install a zipper foot on your machine. Change to a larger needle, if necessary, to accommodate several fabric layers.

Have a fear of zippers? Creating a zipper panel first makes inserting the zipper into a dimensional project a breeze.

4 Place a lining piece and an outer fabric piece from step 1 with wrong sides together, matching the raw edges. Make two stacks. Center the zipper, face down, on one of the outer fabric pieces. The edge of the zipper tape should extend ⅟₁₆" beyond the fabric raw edges, and the raw edges of the tabs should align with the sides of the larger fabric pieces. Sew the zipper to the fabric, ¼" from the fabric edges.

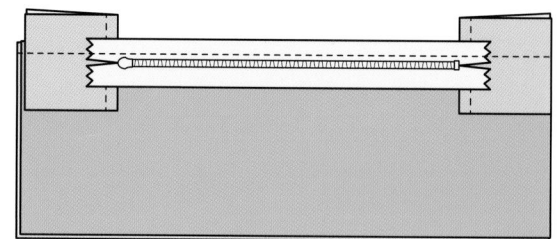

The key to creating ruffles is to first use a long machine stitch.

5 Press the seam allowances and zipper tape toward the fabric and topstitch ⅛" from the seam. Repeat to join the remaining fabric stack to the other side of the zipper. Your zipper panel is ready to incorporate into any project.

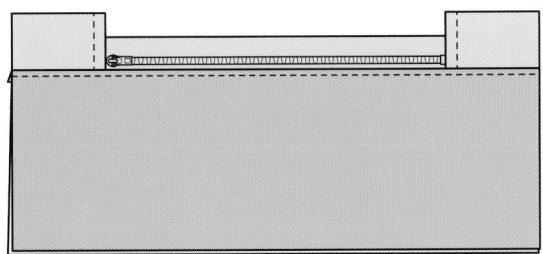

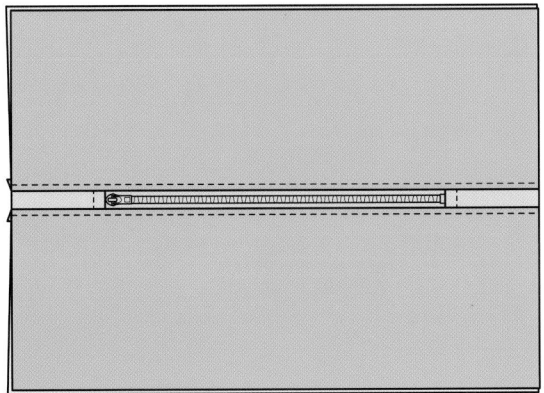

RUFFLE

A ruffle is easy to make by machine basting along the fabric edge and then pulling the bobbin thread to gather the fabric.

1 Cut a strip of fabric as directed in the project instructions and fold it in half lengthwise with wrong sides together.

2 Increase your sewing machine's stitch length to its longest setting. You may also want to loosen the tension of the needle thread slightly. Stitch within the seam allowance along the strip's long raw edge, leaving long tails of both the needle and bobbin threads on each end.

3 Separate the threads at each end and pull the bobbin thread to gather the fabric. Continue pulling, working from each end toward the middle, until the ruffle is the desired length. Adjust gathers as needed so they're evenly distributed along the length of the ruffle.

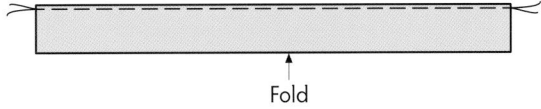

Fold

4 Pin the ruffle to the desired location within your project and sew it in place along the seamline.

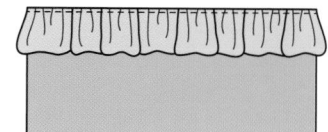

SEAMS

The following two elements are vital for a successful project.

Seam allowances. Throughout the book, seam allowances are ¼" unless stated otherwise.

Pressing. Always press a seam after sewing it; the project instructions will provide directions for pressing the seam allowances open or to one side if the pressing direction is important. Sometimes, when constructing a dimensional project, you'll find it impossible to access a seam for complete pressing. If that happens, finger-press the seam allowances or use a mini iron (or the tip of a regular iron) to press as much of the seam as possible.

PRESSER FEET

A few important presser feet to have for your sewing machine are a ¼" foot, a zipper foot, and a nonstick Teflon-coated foot. The coated foot glides over clingy materials such as laminated cotton, making construction much easier. If you don't have a nonstick presser foot, place a layer of masking tape on the bottom of a standard presser foot as an alternative.

GARDEN GOODNESS

Although the playthings in this garden-themed collection were created with budding "green thumbs" in mind, they also can be reinvented to suit any little one's aspirations. Consider using the gardening bucket as an art-supply caddy, carrying the picnic tote on a trip to the beach, or putting the apron to use in the kitchen.

GARDENING APRON

FINISHED SIZE: 19" x 25" without ties

MATERIALS

Yardage is based on 42"-wide fabric.

1⅛ yards of green laminated cotton for apron body*
1⅛ yards of multicolored print for lining*
½ yard of green gingham for binding
Scraps of assorted cotton prints for appliqués
⅝ yard of green rickrack
½ yard of green ¼"-diameter cording
1 button, 2" diameter
¼ yard of paper-backed fusible web

Yardage allows for cutting the apron and pocket pieces with the lengthwise grain running from top to bottom. If your fabric is nondirectional, you can purchase just ⅞ yard of each fabric and cut the pocket with the long dimension running from side to side.

CUTTING

From the laminated cotton, cut:
1 rectangle, 19" x 25", for apron body
1 rectangle, 10" x 25", for pocket

From the multicolored print, cut:
1 rectangle, 19" x 25", for body lining
1 rectangle, 10" x 25", for pocket lining

From the green gingham, cut:
1½"-wide bias strips totaling 176" when sewn
    together, for binding

APRON BODY

1 Layer the 19" x 25" body and lining rectangles
with wrong sides together and use clips to secure
the edges.

2 Trace the armhole pattern on page 21 to make a
template on paper. Position the template in the
upper-left corner of the stacked rectangles and cut

The "Gardening Apron" offers full coverage and generous pockets plus a no-mess vinyl surface.

along the curved edge. Flip the template over and position it in the upper-right corner of the stacked rectangles. Cut along the curved edge to complete the apron shape.

3 Separate the apron pieces and reserve the lining for
later. Position the rickrack and cording on the apron front as shown, using the project photo for additional guidance. The trims can be curved or positioned in straight lines. Pin the trims to the apron. Sew each trim to the apron with matching thread.

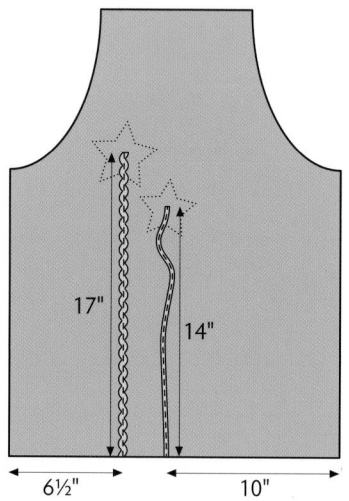

4 Trace two star or flower patterns on page 22 onto the paper side of the fusible web. Use one of each size or combine the shapes as desired. Roughly cut out the shapes and iron the web to the wrong side of the appliqué fabrics. Cut out each shape exactly on the traced outlines. Peel off the paper, position the appliqués on the apron, overlapping the stem ends, and press to fuse. Press from the wrong side of the apron to avoid melting the laminate. Stitch around the appliqué pieces and then sew the button on top of one of the appliquéd shapes.

POCKET

1 Use the gingham bias strips to prepare the binding, referring to "Single-Fold Binding" on page 10.

2 Layer the pocket and pocket lining rectangles with wrong sides together and use clips (see page 8) to secure the edges. Bind the top 25" edge of the pocket with the prepared binding. Trim the binding to match the pocket at the side edges. It's not necessary to finish the binding ends because they'll be covered in a later step.

3 Fold the pocket in half to find the vertical center and finger-press along the folded edge. Mark the upper and lower edges of the pocket as shown to prepare for pleating.

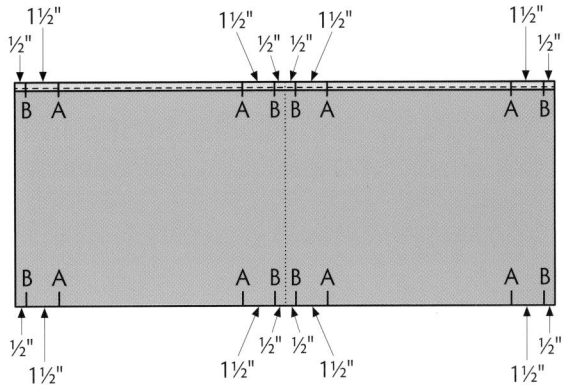

4 Fold the apron body in half to find the vertical center and finger-press along the folded edge. Place the pocket on the apron body, right sides up, matching the center creases and bottom edges. Topstitch the pocket to the apron body along the center crease as shown, backstitching at the pocket's upper edge to reinforce the seam. You'll need to use a nonstick presser foot or cover the bottom of your regular presser foot with masking tape while sewing on the laminated fabric.

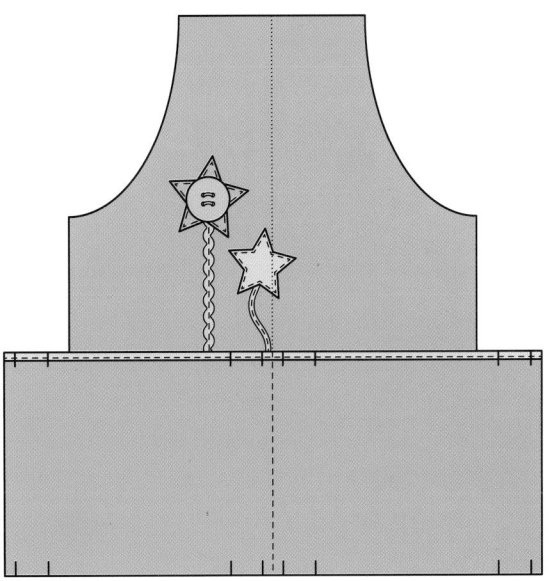

5 Lift the pocket fabric off the apron body and make a vertical fold, wrong sides together, between the two A marks to the left of the center seam. Bring the folded edge to meet the B marks just to the left of center, forming a pleat. Clip the pleat at the upper and lower edges to hold it in place. Repeat to make three more pleats using the remaining A and B marks.

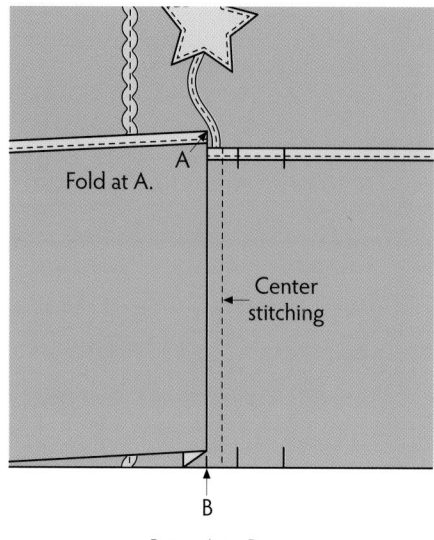

Fold at A.

A

Center stitching

B

Bring A to B.

6 Smooth the pleated pocket back into place on the apron body. The side edges should match; if not, adjust the pleats until they do. Layer the apron lining onto the back of the apron body with wrong sides together. Use clips to hold the edges in place.

FINISHING THE APRON

1 Use the prepared binding to finish the top and bottom edges of the apron. Along the bottom edge, the binding will also secure the pocket pleats.

2 Fold ¼" to the wrong side on one end of the remaining binding. Bind one side of the apron, beginning with the folded end of the binding at the bottom of the apron. Stop sewing and trim the excess binding when you reach the armhole. Repeat this step to bind the other side of the apron.

3 Cut the remaining binding into two equal lengths. Fold ¼" to the wrong side on each end of each piece to create finished edges. Clip one piece of binding to the lower edge of the right armhole 25" from the beginning of the binding; the tail of binding

will form one waist tie. Start sewing at the end of the binding, edgestitching the folded edges of the binding to make a tube. When you reach the armhole at the 25" mark, continue sewing, binding the armhole edge of the apron. At the top of the armhole, continue sewing through the binding only, all the way to the end of the binding, to create one neck tie. Repeat this step to bind the left armhole and make the other two ties. This time you'll need to start sewing with the neck tie; measure the second piece of binding against the first to be sure the ties are the same length.

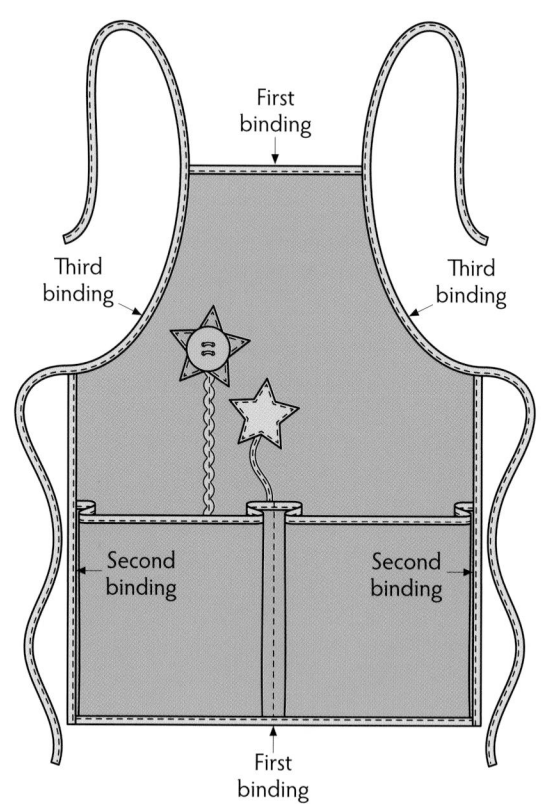

First binding

Third binding

Third binding

Second binding

Second binding

First binding

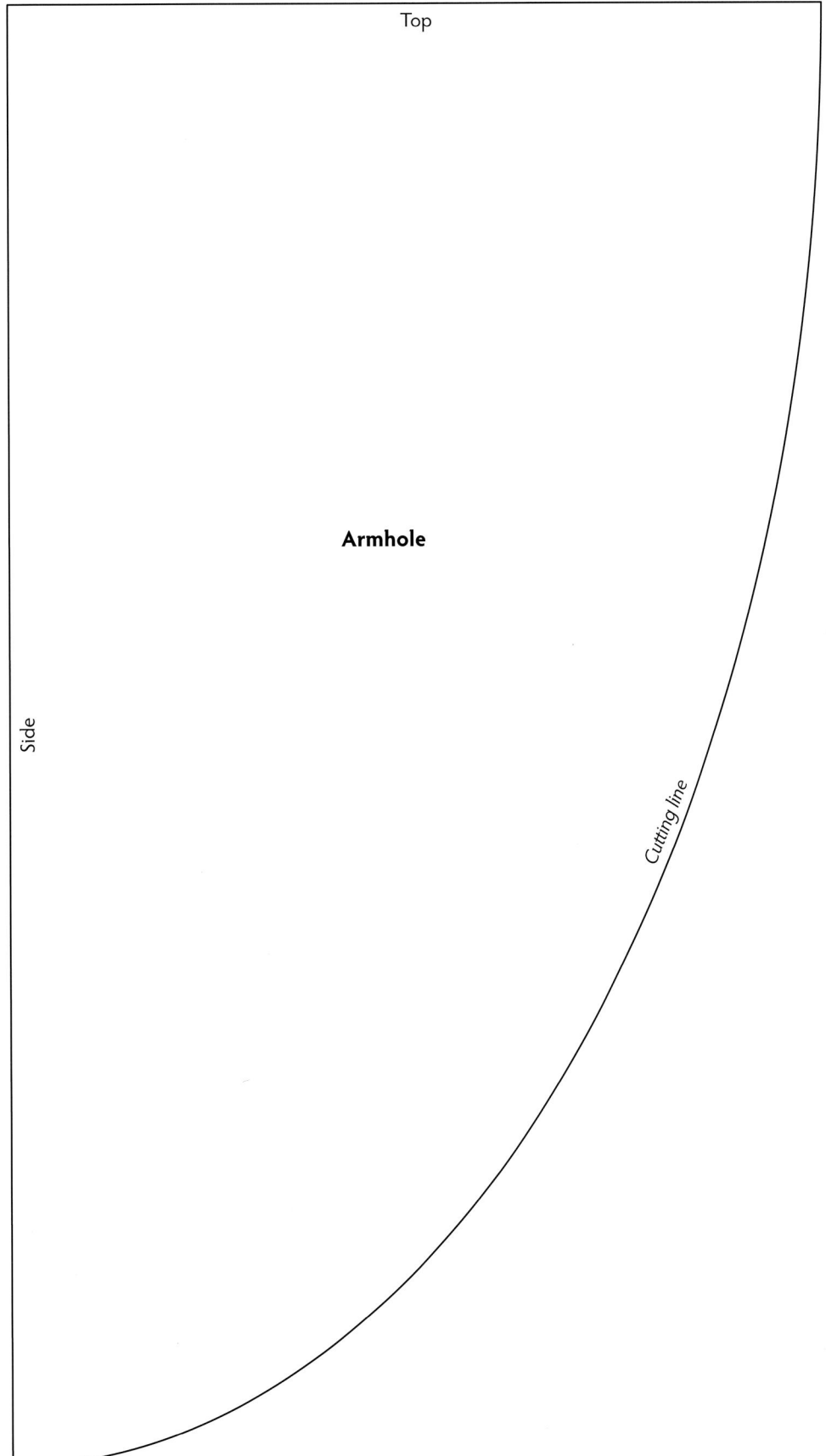

Top

Armhole

Side

Cutting line

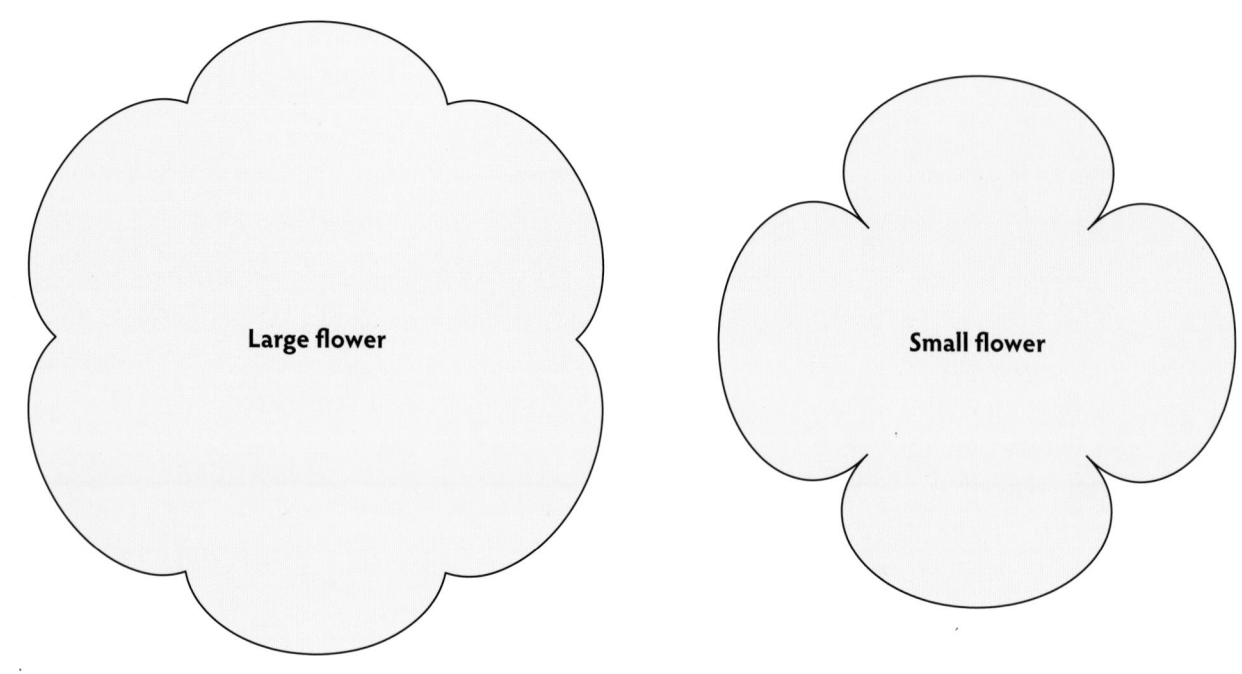

Large flower

Small flower

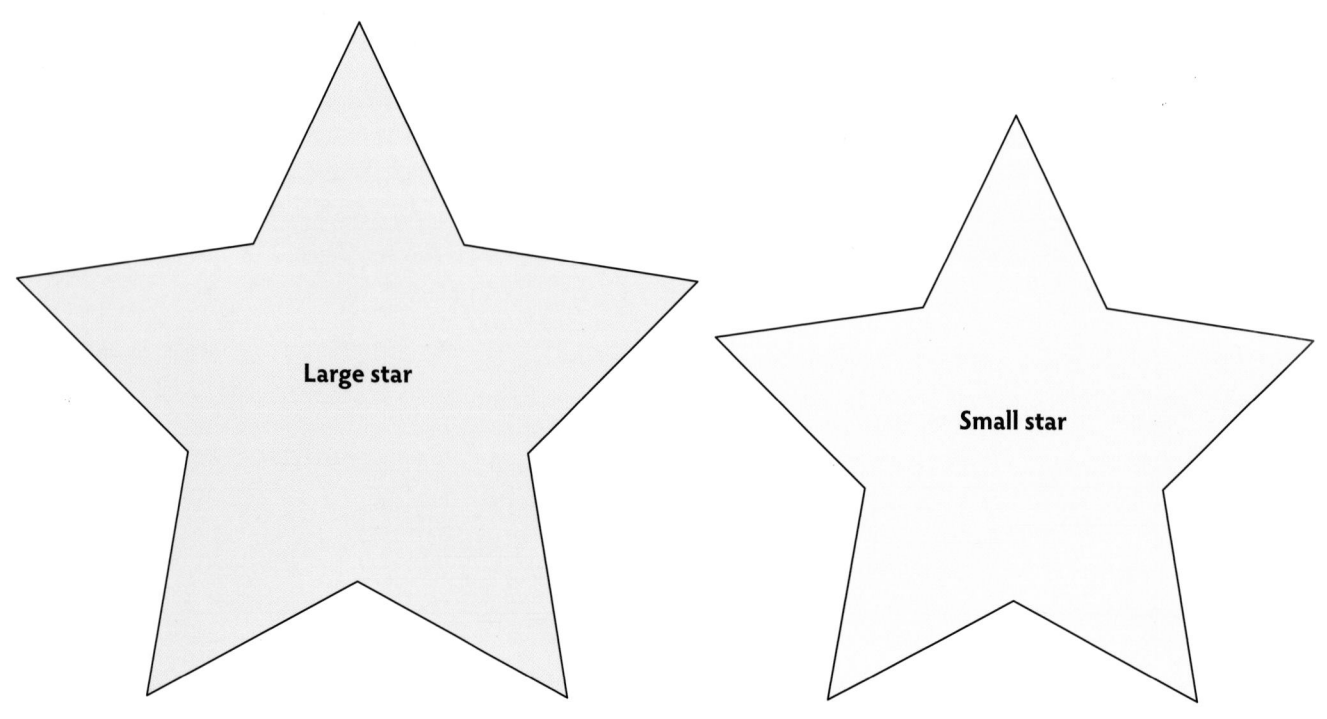

Large star

Small star

GARDENING BUCKET

FINISHED SIZE: 7½" wide x 8¾" high x 7½" deep

MATERIALS

Yardage is based on 42"-wide fabric. Fat quarters measure 18" x 21".

¾ yard of multicolored print for lining
½ yard of natural canvas for body and handles
½ yard of green laminated cotton for pockets
1 fat quarter of turquoise print for base lining
1 fat quarter of turquoise solid for binding
⅔ yard of green ¼"-diameter cording

CUTTING

From the canvas, cut:
4 rectangles, 8" x 9", for bucket body
1 square, 8" x 8", for bucket base
2 rectangles, 4" x 12", for handles

From the multicolored print, cut:
4 rectangles, 8" x 9", for bucket lining
2 rectangles, 6½" x 16", for pocket linings
2 rectangles, 6½" x 8", for side pocket linings

From the turquoise print, cut:
1 square, 8" x 8", for base lining

From the laminated cotton, cut:
2 rectangles, 6½" x 16", for pockets
2 rectangles, 6½" x 8", for side pockets

From the turquoise solid, cut:
1½"-wide bias strips totaling at least 48" when sewn
together, for binding

As wide as it is deep, this handy fabric gardening bucket has lots of functional pocket space.

BUCKET POCKETS

1 Use the turquoise bias strips to prepare the binding, referring to "Single-Fold Binding" on page 10.

2 Place a pocket rectangle on a pocket lining rectangle with wrong sides together and clip to secure the edges. Bind the top 16" edge. Make two. Repeat with the side pockets and their linings, binding one 8" edge of each.

3 Fold each 16" pocket in half to find the vertical center and finger-press a crease. Repeat this process with two of the 8" x 9" canvas rectangles, making the crease parallel to the 9" sides. Mark the upper and lower edges of each 16" pocket as shown to prepare for pleating.

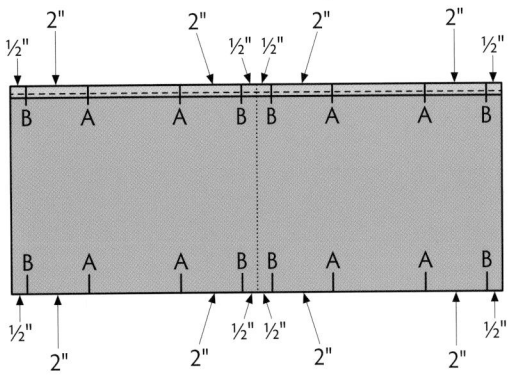

4 Place a pocket on a bucket-body rectangle, right sides up, matching the lower edges and center creases. Topstitch the pocket to the body along the center crease as shown, backstitching at the pocket's upper edge to reinforce the seam. You will need to use a nonstick presser foot or cover the bottom of your regular presser foot with masking tape while sewing on the laminated fabric.

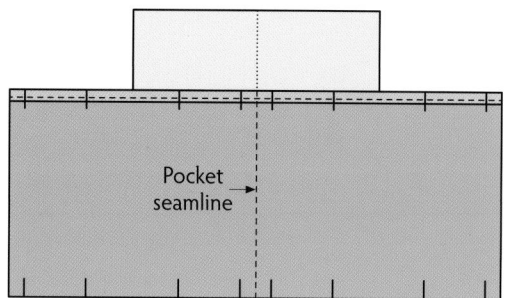

Pocket seamline

5 Lift the pocket fabric off the bucket body and make a vertical fold, wrong sides together, between the first A marks to the left of the center seam. Bring the folded edge to meet the B marks just to the left of center, forming a pleat. Clip the pleat at the upper and lower edges to hold it in place. Repeat to make three more pleats using the remaining A and B marks.

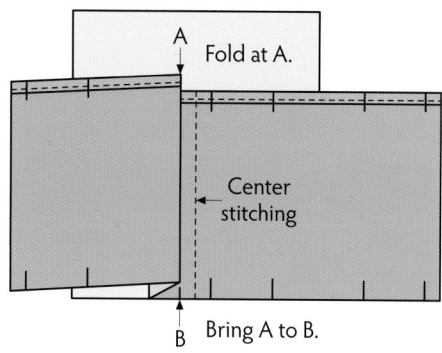

A Fold at A.

Center stitching

B Bring A to B.

Neat Pleats

Although the pleats will be stitched in place only along the bottom edge, marking and folding the pleats all the way to the upper edge yields a neater finish.

6 Smooth the pleated pocket back into place on the bucket body. The side edges should match; if not, adjust the pleats until they do. Repeat from step 4 to make a second bucket-body unit.

7 Place a side-pocket unit on each remaining bucket body, right sides up, matching the side and lower edges. Use clips to hold the pieces together.

BUCKET BODY

1 Arrange the base and bucket units as shown. Sew each unit to the base, beginning and ending the seams ¼" from the raw edges and backstitching at each end.

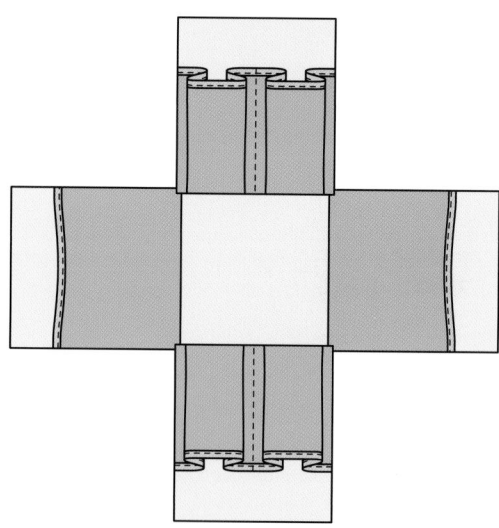

2 Sew the side seams, stitching from the seam intersection at the base to the top edge of the bucket. Backstitch at each end of the seams. Press the side seam allowances open and press the base seam allowances to one side.

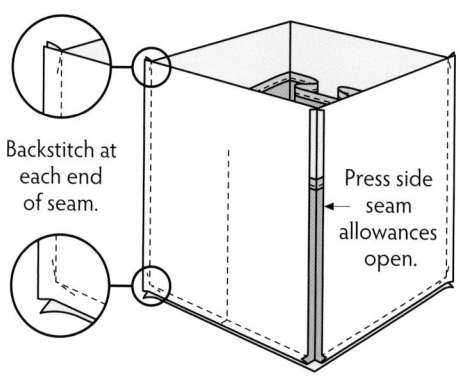

Backstitch at each end of seam.

Press side seam allowances open.

Kids will find plenty of options for storing treasures in this multi-pocketed piece.

BUCKET LINING

Sew the lining, using the same directions for assembling the outer body, with two exceptions: omit references to the pockets, and leave a 4" gap in one seam joining the base to a side rectangle for turning.

HANDLES AND TIES

1 Fold a handle strip in half lengthwise with right sides together. Sew the long raw edge and press the seam allowances open. Turn the handle right side out and press it flat, centering the seam on the handle. Make two.

2 Measure and mark each handle 3" from each end. Fold a handle in half lengthwise with the seam inside the fold and clip in place between the marks. Edgestitch the 6" segment of handle between the marks to shape the center of the handle. Repeat with the second handle.

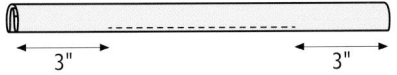

3 Position the ends of one handle on one of the bucket panels with pleated pockets, matching the raw edges. The side edge of the handle should lie next to the bucket side seam, with the seamed surface of the handle facing away from the bucket. Baste the handle ends to the bucket, ⅛" from the raw edges. Repeat to position and baste the second handle on the other bucket panel with pleated pockets.

4 Cut two 10" pieces of the cording. Pin one piece to each of the bucket panels with pleated pockets, centering the cording along the top edge between the handle ends. Baste the cording in place ⅛" from the raw edges.

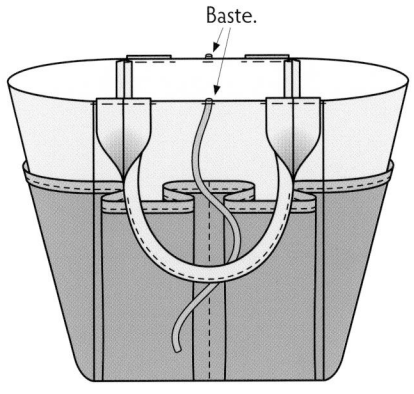

FINISHING THE BUCKET

1 Turn the bucket right side out; leave the lining wrong side out. Slip the lining over the bucket with right sides together. Tuck the handles and ties between the layers so they will be out of the way. Sew along the top edge of the bucket, catching the ends of the handles and ties.

2 Turn the project right side out through the opening in the lining seam. Tuck the lining inside the bucket and press the top edge flat.

3 Press the seam allowances to the wrong side along the gap in the lining. Match the pressed edges and close the opening by either topstitching ⅛" from the pressed edges or sewing invisibly by hand.

4 Topstitch ¼" from the top of the bucket.

PICNIC BLANKET

FINISHED SIZE: 40" x 40"

MATERIALS

Yardage is based on 42"-wide fabric.

1¼ yards of green laminated cotton for blanket top
1¼ yards of multicolored stripe for backing
⅜ yard of turquoise print for binding
40" x 40" square of batting

CUTTING

From the laminated cotton, cut:
1 square, 40" x 40"

From the striped print, cut:
1 square, 40" x 40"

From the turquoise print, cut:
5 strips, 2½" x 42"

MAKING THE BLANKET

1 Layer the backing fabric, wrong side up, followed by the batting and then the laminated cotton, right side up, to form a quilt sandwich.

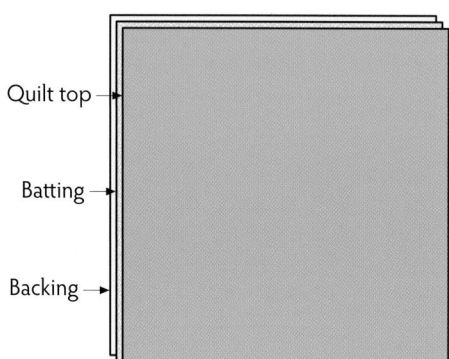

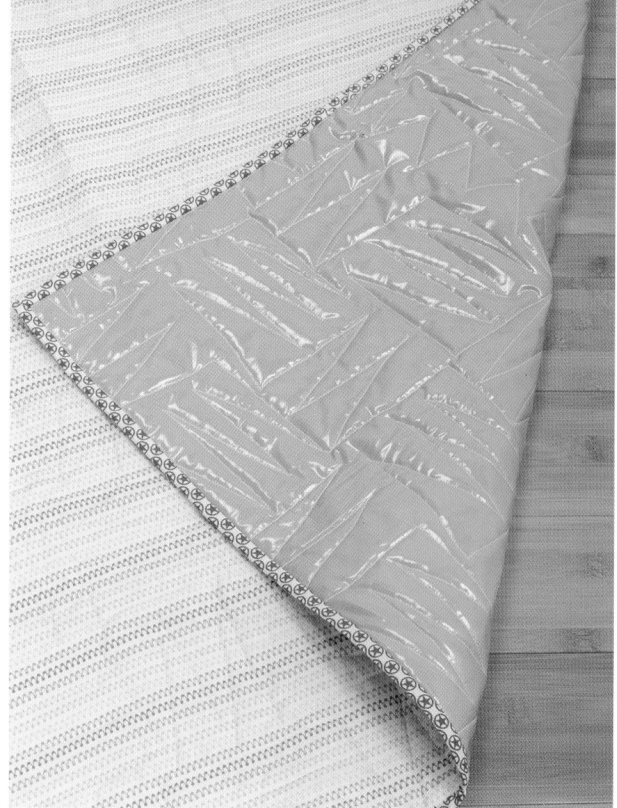

This quick and easy picnic blanket is perfect for outdoor play.

2 Quilt the layers together as desired. I used my long-arm machine to quilt the blanket with a blocky pattern of zigzags. A free-motion quilting foot works well with laminated fabrics because the foot makes minimal contact with the fabric. If you prefer machine-guided straight-line quilting, use a coated foot that will glide over the laminated cotton.

3 Trim the sides of the quilt if necessary.

FINISHING THE BLANKET

1 Join and press the binding strips as described in "Double-Fold Binding" on page 12.

2 Bind the blanket with the prepared binding strip, mitering the corners.

PICNIC TOTE

FINISHED SIZE: 10½" wide x 16" high x 3½" deep

MATERIALS

Yardage is based on 42"-wide fabric. Fat quarters measure 18" x 21".

½ yard of natural canvas for body
½ yard of blue print for lining
¼ yard of green laminated cotton for contrast
⅛ yard of turquoise solid for ties

CUTTING

From the canvas, cut:
4 rectangles, 6½" x 12½", for body
1 rectangle, 4" x 11", for base

From the blue print, cut:
4 rectangles, 6½" x 16½", for lining
1 rectangle, 4" x 11", for base lining
1 square, 6½" x 6½", for pocket lining
1 rectangle, 3" x 24", for strap

From the laminated cotton, cut:
1 rectangle, 4½" x 24½", for contrasting band
1 square, 6½" x 6½", for pocket
1 rectangle, 3" x 24", for strap

From the turquoise solid, cut:
1 strip, 1½" x 42", for binding

TOTE POCKET

1 Layer the laminated cotton and blue-print pocket pieces with right sides together. Sew along the top edge.

2 Press the seam open, and then fold the pocket along the seam with wrong sides together, matching the raw edges, and press again. Topstitch ¼" from the seam (see illustration at right).

The picnic blanket fits nicely into this little picnic tote. There's plenty of room for picnic goodies, too.

3 Position the pocket on one canvas body piece, matching the side and lower edges, and clip in place.

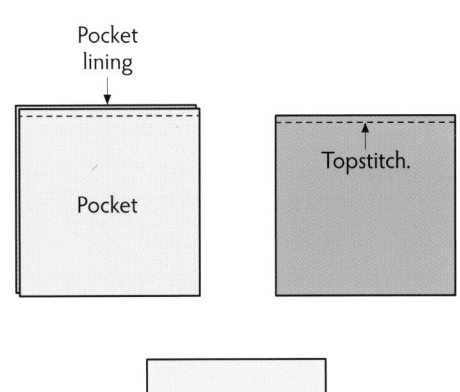

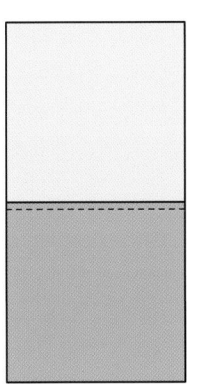

TOTE STRAP

1 Layer the laminated-cotton and blue-print strap pieces with right sides together. Sew along each 24" side to make a tube. Turn the tube right side out and press from the fabric side with the seams along the sides of the strap.

2 Topstitch ¼" from the seamed edges. Sew with the laminated fabric on top and use a nonstick presser foot to avoid drag.

TOTE BODY

1 Use the pattern on page 29 to make a template for rounding the base ends.

2 Place the template on one end of the bag base and trace the curved edge. Remove the template and cut along the traced line. Repeat to round the other end of the piece. Repeat the step to shape the ends of the base lining.

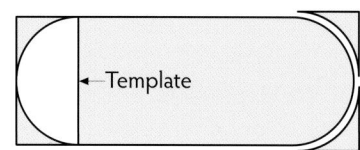

Template

3 Fold the contrasting band in half, wrong sides together, and sew the 4½" ends together to create a ring. Fold the band in half along the seam to find the center point and mark it with a removable marker or tiny clip into the seam allowance; mark both long edges. Refold, matching the mark to the seam line, and mark the two new folds in the same way, dividing the ring into quarters.

4 Sew the four tote body pieces together along their 12½" sides to make a ring. Fold each canvas panel in half to find its midpoint and mark each one along the bottom edge.

5 With right sides together, use clips to hold the contrasting band to the canvas unit. Position the contrasting band's seam at the midpoint of the bag back (the piece opposite the one with the pocket). Match the remaining marks on the band to the midpoints of the other bag panels. Sew the band to the bag and finger-press the seam to one side.

6 Find the center of the upper edge of the bag back. Center the strap, laminated side up, on the right side of the bag with raw edges matched. Baste ⅛" from the raw edges.

7 Repeat step 6 to baste the free end of the strap to the bottom edge of the bag, centering the strip on the seam in the laminated-cotton band.

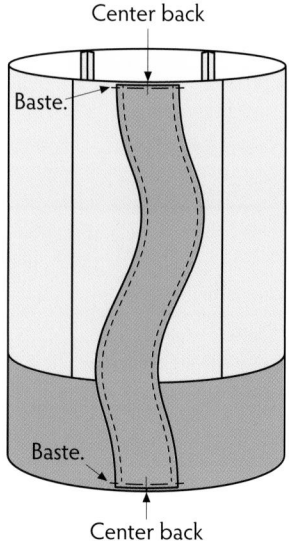

Center back

Baste.

Baste.

Center back

8 Fold the canvas base piece in half in each direction to find and mark the centers of each side and end. Use clips to attach the canvas base to the free edge of the laminated-cotton band, matching the quarter marks on the two pieces, with the strap end between the bag and base. Sew the pieces together and finger-press the seam allowances to one side.

9 Use the turquoise strip to prepare the binding, referring to "Single-Fold Binding" on page 10. Cut two pieces, 13" long, for ties. Temporarily open the folded bias and press ¼" to the wrong side on one end of each tie. Refold the ties and sew along the long open edge and pressed end.

10 Position the ties on the top edge of the bag, matching the raw edges. Place one tie along each seam connecting the front panel to a side panel. Baste ⅛" from the raw edges.

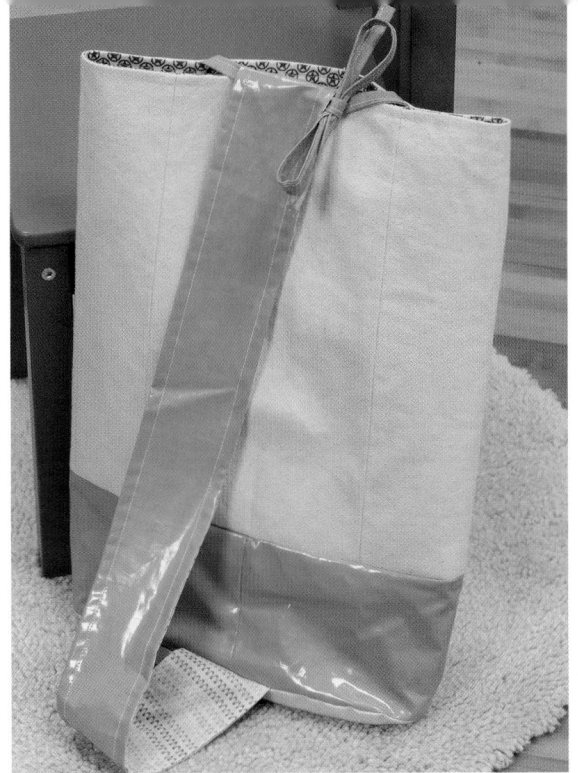

TOTE LINING

1 Sew the four lining panels together to make a ring. Find and mark the center of each panel along its lower edge.

2 Fold and mark the lining base as in step 8 of "Tote Body." Pin or clip the base to the lining panels, matching the center marks, and sew, leaving a 4" opening along the straightest part of the seam. Press the seam allowances to one side.

FINISHING THE TOTE

1 Turn the outer body right side out; leave the lining wrong side out. Slip the lining over the body with right sides together, matching the seams. Be sure the handles and ties are tucked between the layers, out of the way. Stitch along the top edge.

2 Turn the project right side out through the gap in the lining seam. Press the seam allowances to the wrong side along the gap. Close the opening by either topstitching ⅛" from the pressed edges or sewing invisibly by hand.

3 Topstitch ¼" from the top edge of the tote, keeping the strap free.

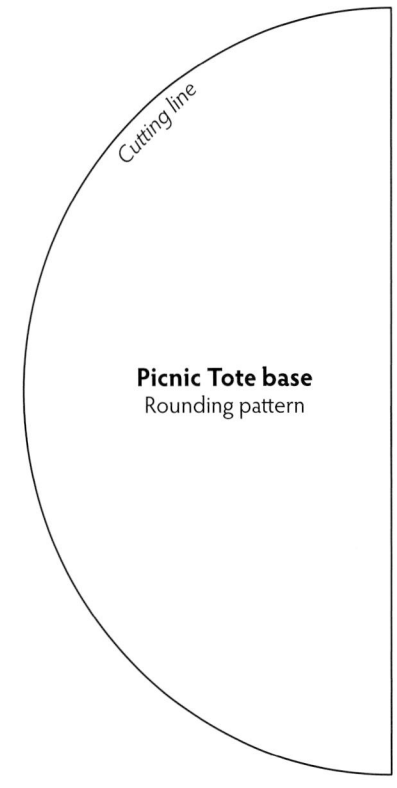

Cutting line

Picnic Tote base
Rounding pattern

SHOP'S OPEN

Make-believe shopkeeping is fun with this well-stocked collection of supplies, including a play shop, task apron, and shopping basket. Consider using the store as a restaurant, flower stand, bike shop, or fabric shop!

TASK APRON

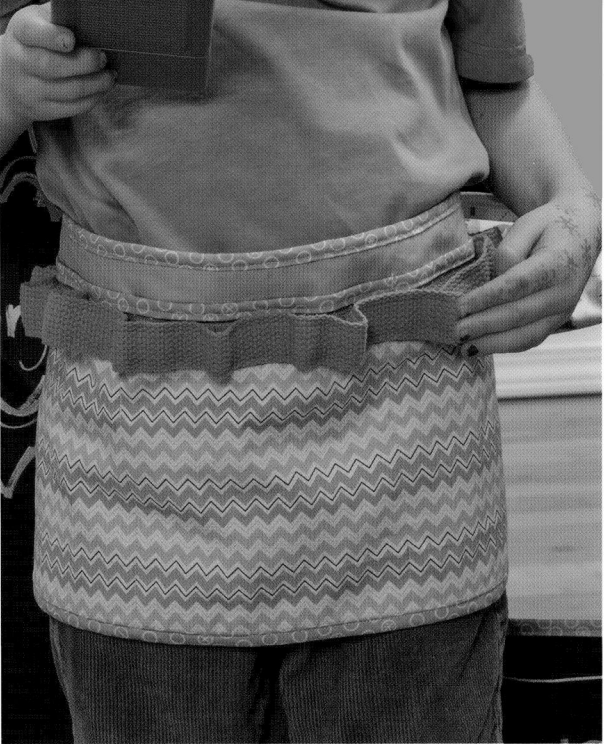

FINISHED SIZE: 8" x 18" without belt

MATERIALS

Fat quarters measure 18" x 21".

1 fat quarter of green solid for apron body and
    pocket lining
1 fat quarter of chevron stripe for pocket and
    apron lining
1 fat quarter of turquoise print for binding
1⅞ yards of 1"-wide turquoise webbing
1 yard of ¾"-wide Velcro
1 parachute buckle, 1" wide

CUTTING

From the green solid, cut:
1 rectangle, 8" x 18", for apron body
1 rectangle, 7" x 18", for pocket lining

From the chevron stripe, cut:
1 rectangle, 8" x 18", for apron lining
1 rectangle, 7" x 18", for pocket

From the turquoise print, cut:
1½"-wide bias strips totaling at least 60" when
    sewn together, for binding

Separate the Velcro tapes and cut:
1 piece, 18" long, of the hook tape
1 piece, 28" long, of the loop tape

From the webbing, cut:
1 strip, 28" long
1 strip, 36" long

*Pockets and adjustable tool loops make this apron a handy
helper for any task.*

APRON POCKET

1 Use the turquoise bias strips to prepare the binding,
referring to "Single-Fold Binding" on page 10.

2 Layer the pocket pieces with wrong sides together
and pin or clip the edges. Bind the 18" edge at the
top with the prepared binding strip.

3 Place the 18" strip of Velcro hook on the right side
of the pocket, ¼" below the bias binding.
Edgestitch both long edges of the Velcro to attach it
to the pocket.

4 Layer the apron body pieces with wrong sides
together, matching the raw edges. Place the
pocket on the apron body, right sides up, matching
the side and lower edges, and pin or clip in place.
Draw lines across the pocket from top to bottom, 6"
from each side edge.

Use the Velcro to adjust the loops in the webbing.

The parachute buckle makes the waistband adjustable.

5 Topstitch along each line from the bound upper edge of the pocket to the raw lower edge. Be sure to backstitch at the bound edge, and switch to a larger needle if necessary.

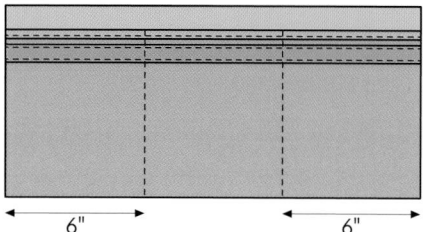

6 Center the 28" strip of Velcro loop on the wrong side of the 28" webbing strip. Edgestitch both long edges of the Velcro to attach it to the webbing. Position the webbing on the pocket's Velcro, matching the raw edges at the sides and distributing the extra length evenly to create hanging loops. Make sure that about ½" of the webbing lies flat against the pocket at each side to facilitate binding the side seams.

Match Game

Match your needle thread to the Velcro color and your bobbin thread to the webbing color to hide your stitches.

APRON BODY

1 Use the pattern on page 33 to make a template. Position the template on the lower-right corner of the stacked apron and pocket pieces. Draw around the curved template edge, remove the template, and cut the fabrics along the line to round the corner. Repeat to round the lower-left corner of the apron.

2 Bind the apron sides and bottom edge with the prepared bias binding.

3 Fold the 36" strip of webbing in half to find its center and mark with a pin. Fold the apron in half and mark the center of its upper edge. Lay the apron

LITTLE BIG STUFF

body, right side up, on top of the webbing, matching the centers and laying the raw edge of the apron along the upper edge of the webbing. Use clips to hold the pieces together.

4 Unfold the end of the bias binding and press ¼" to the wrong side. Refold the binding and press again. Bind the top edge of the apron, slipping the bias binding around the fabrics and webbing. Before you reach the far end of the apron, trim the excess binding ¼" beyond the apron edge, temporarily unfold the binding, and finger-press ¼" to the wrong side of the binding to create a clean finish. Refold the binding and finish stitching it to the apron.

5 To secure the webbing further, topstitch vertically across the webbing ¼" from the apron sides.

FINISHING THE APRON

1 Thread one end of the waistband webbing through the slots on one piece of the parachute buckle. Turn ¼" of the webbing end to the wrong side and press; turn under a second ¼" and press again. Topstitch the hem. If the webbing is too thick for a doubled hem, finish the raw edge with a zigzag stitch and turn the hem under only once.

Use the Big One

The webbing hem will be very thick. Switch to a size 100/16 or larger needle and sew at a slow, steady pace to pierce through all the layers.

2 Repeat step 1 to add the other half of the buckle to the other end of the waistband webbing. Before stitching the hem, be sure the waistband will not be twisted when the buckle is fastened.

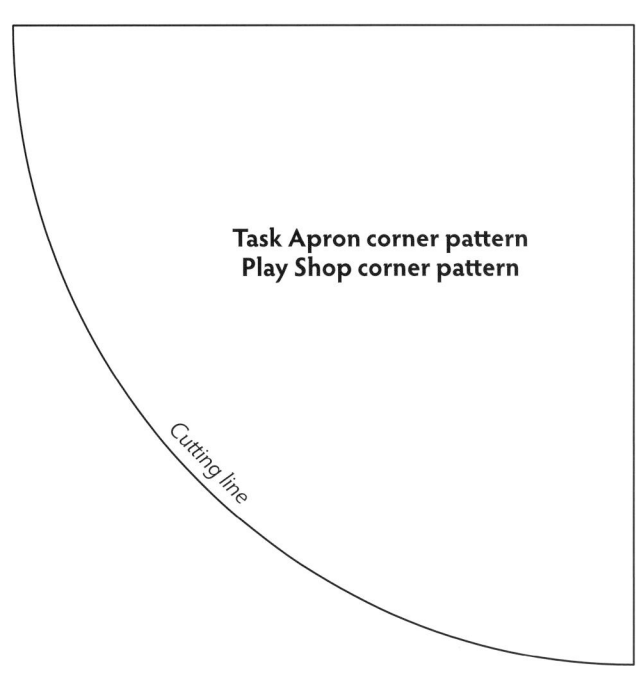

Task Apron corner pattern
Play Shop corner pattern

Cutting line

TASK BASKET

FINISHED SIZE: 15½" wide x 9½" high x 8" deep

MATERIALS

Yardage is based on 42"-wide fabric unless otherwise noted.

1 yard of natural canvas for body
⅞ yard of blue print for contrast and lining
⅓ yard of black 60"-wide sports mesh for pockets
¼ yard of green print for handles and binding
¾ yard of 1"-wide webbing
1 yard of 20"-wide ultra-firm craft interfacing, such as Peltex
Scrap of chalkboard fabric (optional)
3" scrap of blue rickrack (optional)

CUTTING

From the natural canvas, cut:
2 rectangles, 14" x 24", for basket body
1 rectangle, 8" x 24", for outside pocket lining
1 rectangle, 8½" x 18", for floating pocket

From the blue print, cut:
4 rectangles, 12½" x 14", for basket lining
1 rectangle, 8" x 24", for outside pocket
1 rectangle, 8½" x 18", for floating pocket

From the sports mesh, cut:
1 rectangle, 8" x 28", for outer pocket

From the green print, cut:
4 rectangles, 2" x 12", for handles
1½"-wide bias strips totaling at least 28" when sewn together, for binding

From the webbing, cut:
2 strips, 12" long

From the interfacing, cut:
3 strips, 9½" x 20"

This task or shopping basket sits open for easy loading and unloading.

BASKET OUTER POCKETS

1 Use the green bias strips to prepare the binding, referring to "Single-Fold Binding" on page 10. Bind one 28" edge of the mesh pocket.

2 Measure and mark the 28" edges of the mesh pocket 6" and 8" from each end, as shown. Fold the mesh with wrong sides together at each 8" mark, and bring the fold to meet the nearest 6" mark. Pin or clip the edges to hold the pleats in place.

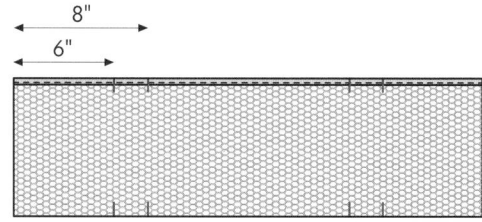

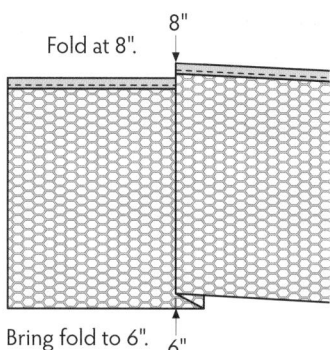

Fold at 8".

8"

Bring fold to 6".   6"

3 Place the canvas and blue print outside pockets with right sides together, matching the edges. Sew one of the 24" sides; this will be the top of the pocket.

4 Separate the pocket layers along the open 24" edge. Place the pleated mesh pocket on the print pocket, with the wrong side of the mesh against the right side of the print. Match the raw edges. If necessary, adjust the pleats in the mesh pocket for a correct fit. Smooth the canvas pocket back onto the print pocket, right sides together, with the mesh in between, and pin or clip. Sew the remaining 18" edge. Turn the pocket right side out and press the canvas and print pocket flat along the seams, keeping the mesh pocket out of the way. Topstitch ¼" from each seam through the print and canvas layers only.

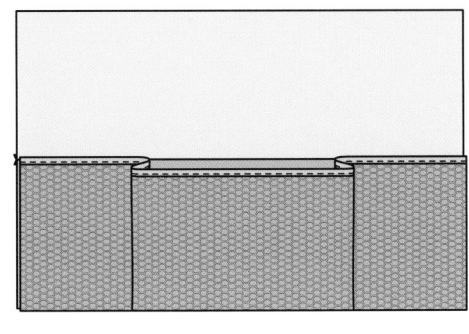

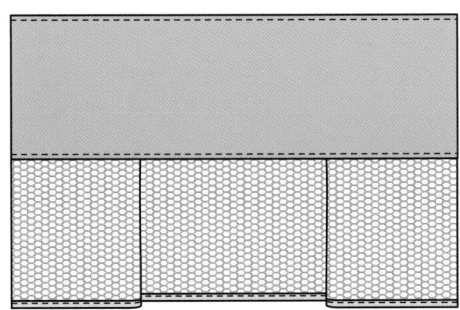

5 Temporarily fold the mesh onto the print side of the pocket, right side up, and pin or clip the side edges. Fold the basket body and pocket unit in half to find the vertical centers and finger-press both to mark the centers. Place the pocket unit on the basket body with its upper edge 2" below the top of the basket, matching the centers. Fold the mesh down and out of the way. Topstitch ¼" from the bottom of the pocket, on top of the previous stitches, to join the pocket to the basket. Flip the mesh up into place and topstitch through all the layers along the finger-pressed centerline.

6 For the optional label, cut a 2" x 3" scrap of chalkboard fabric. Cut and prepare an additional 12" of bias binding, and use it to finish the edges. Topstitch a scrap of rickrack to the top of the chalkboard label. Topstitch the label to the basket, centered ¼" below the top of the pocket.

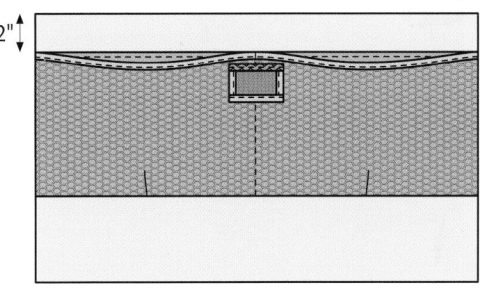

BASKET ASSEMBLY

1 Layer the basket body pieces (front with pockets and back without) with right sides together and sew the side and bottom edges. Be sure the outside pockets open toward the top of the basket. Press the seam allowances open.

2 Fold the basket so the bottom seam aligns with one side seam, forming a triangular point. Measure along the seam and mark a perpendicular line 4" from the point; this line should fall at or just below the bottom of the pocket. Sew on the marked line. Cut away the excess fabric, leaving ¼" seam allowances. Repeat the entire step to box the remaining corner.

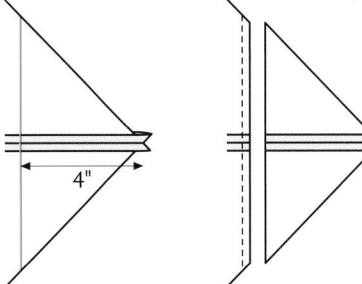

BASKET HANDLES

1 Layer two handle rectangles with right sides together. Sew along both 12" sides. Turn right side out and press the handle flat with the seams along the sides. Center a piece of webbing on the handle and edgestitch the webbing to the fabric handle. Make two.

2 Measure 3" from both sides of each side seam and mark with pins. Position a handle across one side seam, with the handle ends at the 3" marks. The fabric side of the handle should lie against the right side of the basket fabric, with the raw edges matched. Baste ⅛" from the raw edges. Repeat to baste the second handle to the other side of the basket.

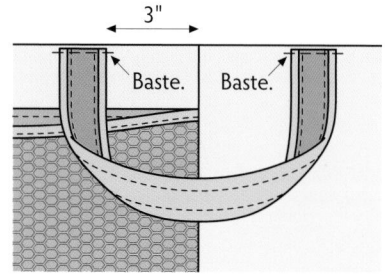

FLOATING POCKET AND LINING

1 Layer the floating pocket pieces with right sides together and sew along both 8½" sides. Turn the pocket right side out and press flat. Topstitch ¼" from each seam. Fold the pocket in half with the canvas inside, matching the topstitched edges at the top of the pocket and the raw edges along the sides. The fold will be the bottom of the pocket.

2 Lay the floating pocket along one 14" edge of a lining rectangle with right sides up and the top of the pocket ½" below the top edge of the lining. Place another lining rectangle on top so that the two lining pieces are right sides together with the pocket sandwiched between them. Sew the pieces together along the 14" edge that includes the pocket. Press the seam allowances open. Open out the lining pieces so that the pocket stands up between them.

The task basket can double as a storage basket when play time is over.

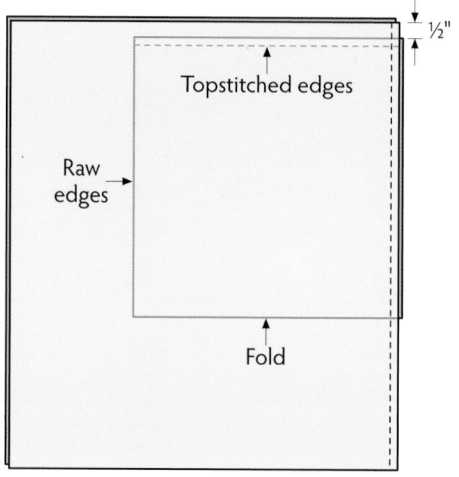

A center divider creates compartments inside the basket.

Mesh pockets make room for little extras.

3 Repeat step 2 to sew the remaining raw edges of the floating pocket between the remaining two basket-lining rectangles. Seen from the top, the lining unit will have an H shape, with the floating pocket forming the horizontal bar.

4 Treat each leg of the H as one lining panel; sew the side and bottom seams. Leave an 8" gap in the bottom seam for turning. As you stitch the bottom seam, be sure not to confuse the side seams with the seams holding the floating pocket. Box the corners as you did in step 2 of "Basket Assembly."

5 Join the strips of ultra-firm interfacing to make one long piece. To do this, lay two pieces side by side with their 9½" edges abutting. Set the machine for a wide zigzag stitch and sew the pieces of interfacing together, allowing the needle to swing back and forth from one piece to the other. From the joined interfacing, cut a 47" length. Sew the ends together to create a ring of interfacing.

FINISHING THE BASKET

1 Turn the basket right side out; leave the lining wrong side out. Slip the lining over the basket with right sides together. The floating pocket may make this awkward, but as long as the raw edges at the top are aligned, the remainder of the project doesn't have to be smooth. Be sure the handles are tucked between the shell and lining, out of the way. Sew along the top edge.

2 Turn the project right side out through the opening in the lining seam. Tuck the lining inside the basket and press the top edge. Slip the ultra-firm interfacing through the gap used for turning and position it between the side walls of the body and lining. Slide the interfacing all the way up to the top seam.

3 Topstitch ¼" from the top edge, catching the interfacing in the stitches to hold it in place. Close the gap in the lining by hand or machine.

PLAY SHOP

FINISHED SIZE: 36" wide x 28" high x 36" deep

MATERIALS

Yardage is based on 42"-wide fabric unless otherwise noted.

3¼ yards of 48"-wide chalkboard fabric
½ yard of blue print for binding
1 yard of multicolored print for curtains
1⅞ yards of ¾"-wide black Velcro

CUTTING

From the chalkboard fabric, cut:
3 rectangles, 28" x 36½", for shop front and sides
36 squares, 6½" x 6½", for roof

From the blue print, cut:
1½"-wide bias strips totaling at least 390" when
    sewn together, for binding

From the multicolored print, cut:
4 squares, 12" x 12", for side curtains
1 rectangle, 12" x 18", for front curtain

Separate the Velcro tapes and cut:
3 pieces, 12" long, of the hook tape
4 pieces, 12" long, of the loop tape
1 piece, 18" long, of the loop tape

Turn a card table into a thriving place of busy-ness with a fun-to-make chalkboard fabric cover.

OPEN SHOP ASSEMBLY

The open shop consists of three side panels and a roof. It's sized to fit over a 36"-square table, creating a perfect play space; hard-top tables are the best, for durability. Each side panel has a window cutout, and the edges are bound before the panels are joined. Refer to the illustrations as a guide for placement of the windows and binding as you work through the step-by-step instructions.

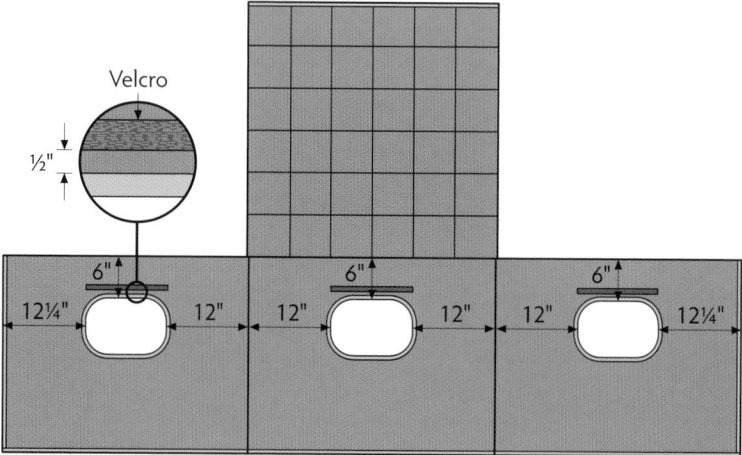

1 Use the blue bias strips to prepare the binding, referring to "Single-Fold Binding" on page 10.

2 Sew the 6½" squares together in six rows of six squares each to create a 36½" x 36½" roof. Use the prepared bias binding to bind one edge of the roof; this will be the back edge.

3 You'll cut an 8" x 12" window from each panel. To begin, establish one 36½" edge of each panel as the top. Measure 6" from the top and draw a horizontal line on the front panel. Measure and draw lines 12¼" from each side edge to create the sides of an 8" x 12" rectangle. Draw a second horizontal line, 8" below the first, to complete the window rectangle.

Easy Writer

A bonus when working on chalkboard fabric: marking and erasing locations is easy when you're doing it with chalk!

4 Make a template from the pattern on page 33. Position the template in one corner of the window rectangle and draw around the curved edge. Erase the straight lines at the corner. Repeat to round the other three corners of the window. Cut out the fabric in the center of the window rectangle. Bind the window opening with prepared bias binding. Center a 12" length of Velcro hook ½" above the window and edgestitch it in place.

5 Repeat steps 2–4 to make windows in the two side panels.

6 Sew the panels together along their 28" sides with the front panel between the two side panels. Bind the free 28" edge of each side panel, and then bind the entire lower edge. Turn ¼" to the wrong side at each end of the binding to create a clean finish.

7 Matching their centers, sew the front panel to the edge of the roof opposite the bound edge. The seamlines between panels lie ¼" from the edges of the roof; stop sewing at the seamlines.

8 Sew each side panel to the corresponding roof edge, stitching from the ends of the front-panel seam to the bound back edges.

MAKING THE CURTAINS

1 Use the pattern on page 33 to round the bottom corners of all the curtain pieces. For the front curtain, use one 18" edge as the top.

2 Bind the side and bottom edges of each curtain piece, easing the binding around the curves.

3 Sew a matching length of Velcro loop tape to the wrong side of each curtain piece, matching the edge of the Velcro to the top edge of the curtain. Edgestitch the lower edge of the Velcro to the curtain fabric. Bind the top edge of each curtain piece, catching the Velcro in the binding. Turn under ¼" at each end of the binding to create a clean finish.

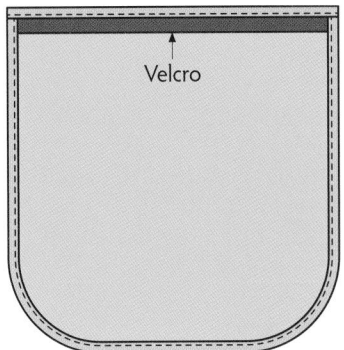

Velcro

4 Optional: Use the remaining binding to create six curtain ties, each 10" long, by sewing the open edges of the binding together. Sew the centers of two ties to the top of the front window. Sew the center of one tie to each side of each side window. Use hand stitches to secure the ties, or machine stitch back and forth over the ties to hold them in place on the shop panels.

5 Use the Velcro fasteners to attach the curtains to the windows, ruffling the curtain fabric to create a gathered look. Roll up the front curtain and secure it with the curtain ties when the shop is open for business. Use the ties on the side windows to hold the curtain panels in place.

CAMPOUT FUN

Whether for campouts, sleepovers, or special nights at a grandparent's house, this collection offers the go-to gear every little adventurer will reach for again and again. Let's get sewing!

SLEEPING BAG

FINISHED SIZE: 30" x 60"

MATERIALS

Yardage is based on 42"-wide fabric.

3½ yards *total* of assorted prints for sleeping bag

4⅜ yards of brown-print flannel for lining, binding, and ties

2 yards of ¾"-wide Velcro

1¼ yards of ½"-wide elastic

68" x 68" piece of wool batting

68" x 68" piece of polyester and cotton blend batting

CUTTING

From the assorted prints, cut a *total* of:

144 squares, 5½" x 5½"

From the brown-print flannel, cut:

2 rectangles, 34¼" x 68", for lining*

4 rectangles, 6½" x 12", for ties

2 rectangles, 2" x 30", for elastic straps

6 strips, 2½" x 42", for binding

From the elastic, cut:

2 pieces, 20" long

From the Velcro, cut:

1 piece, 30" long

1 piece, 40" long

*For efficient fabric use, cut the large rectangles first and then cut the remaining pieces from the leftover fabric.

SLEEPING BAG

1 Arrange the 5½" squares randomly in 12 rows of 12 squares each. Sew the squares together in rows. Press the seam allowances to one side, alternating the direction from row to row. Join the rows and press the seam allowances in one direction.

2 Sew the two 34¼" x 68" flannel rectangles together to make a 68" square and press the seam

For rest time or play, this sleeping bag is as cozy as it is cute.

allowances open. If you haven't removed the selvages, position the selvages on the outer edges where they will be trimmed later.

3 Create a sandwich from the lining, wrong side up; the two layers of batting; and the pieced shell, right side up. Quilt as desired; the sample is quilted with an allover looping pattern. Trim the backing and batting layers to match the pieced shell.

Simple Stitches

Stitch a simple grid by making an "X" through each square to quilt the layers.

TIES, STRAPS, AND VELCRO

1 The ties are made like binding, so refer to "Single-Fold Binding" on page 10 for details. After pressing, temporarily unfold each tie and press ¼" to the wrong side on one end. Refold, press, and topstitch ⅛" from all three finished edges of the tie. Make four.

Elastic straps make it easy for small hands to close a bed roll.

2 Decide which edge of the quilted bag will be the top. Mark the lining along each side edge, 5¼" and 15¼" from the top; the marks will fall along seamlines between patches. Position the raw edges of a tie on the sleeping bag lining at each mark, matching the raw edges. Baste the ties to the sleeping bag ⅛" from the raw edges.

3 Separate the two halves of each Velcro length. Referring to the illustration, position the Velcro tapes ⅛" from the edges of the sleeping bag on the lining side. They will be partially covered later by the binding. Place the 40" lengths of Velcro along the sides of the sleeping bag and the 30" lengths along the bottom edge. Edgestitch the Velcro to the sleeping bag.

4 Each strap is a fabric tube with elastic inside. Fold a strap rectangle in half lengthwise with right sides together. Sew the long edge and then turn the tube right side out. Press the tube flat with the seam along one edge. Thread one piece of elastic through the tube, using a safety pin clipped to the leading edge. Use a second safety pin, if desired, to keep the end of the elastic from being drawn into the tube. Match the ends of the elastic to the ends of the fabric tube and stitch ⅛" from the raw edges on each end of the strap to hold the elastic in place. Make two.

5 Fold each strap in half, matching the raw edges. Position the straps on the sleeping bag shell along the lower edge, 5¼" and 10¼" from the lower-left corner. To reduce bulk, arrange the strap ends so they lie side by side, centered on the seamlines between patches. Baste the straps to the sleeping bag ⅛" from the raw edges.

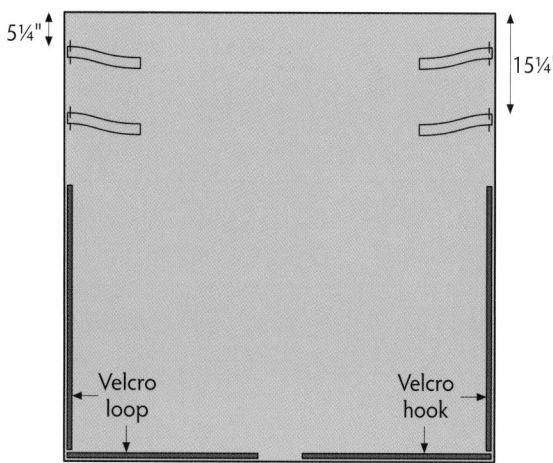

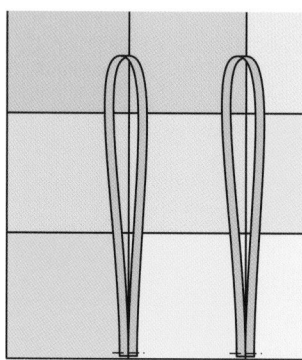

FINISHING THE SLEEPING BAG

1 Prepare the binding as directed in "Double-Fold Binding" on page 12.

2 Bind the edges of the sleeping bag, catching the Velcro, ties, and straps in the binding seam.

PILLOW

FINISHED SIZE: 16" x 12"

MATERIALS

Yardage is based on 42"-wide fabric.

½ yard of brown polka-dot flannel for pillow
⅛ yard of tan print for binding
12" x 16" pillow form

CUTTING

From the brown flannel, cut:
1 rectangle, 12½" x 16½", for pillow front
2 rectangles, 9" x 16½", for pillow backs

From the tan print, cut:
1 strip, 1½" x 36", for binding

MAKING THE PILLOW

1 Prepare binding from the tan strip, referring to "Single-Fold Binding" on page 10.

2 Bind one long edge of each pillow back.

3 Layer the pillow front and backs with right sides together. Overlap the bound edges of the pillow backs so that the raw edges match around the entire pillow.

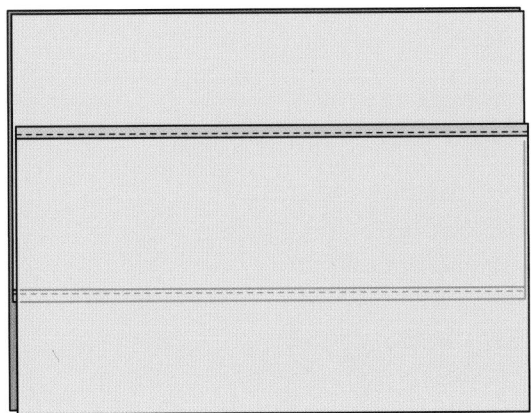

This small pillow is a comfy companion for camping, traveling, or napping.

4 Sew the entire outer edge of the pillow. Clip the corners diagonally to reduce bulk and turn the pillow right side out through the bound edges. Smooth the corners into shape.

5 Insert the pillow form through the opening in the pillow back.

Fill a Form

If you're unable to find a 12" x 16" pillow form or you simply prefer to make your own, purchase ⅜ yard of muslin and a bag of polyester fiberfill. Cut two 12½" x 16½" rectangles from the muslin. Sew them with right sides together, leaving a small opening for turning. Clip the corners diagonally to reduce bulk, turn the pillow form right side out, and stuff with the fiberfill. Slipstitch the opening by hand.

DUFFEL BAG

FINISHED SIZE: 15¼" wide x 10½" high x 7¼" deep

MATERIALS

Yardage is based on 42"-wide fabric.

1 yard *total* of assorted prints for shell*
1 yard of natural canvas for interlining
1 yard of brown-print flannel for lining
⅝ yard of tan print for base and piping
¼ yard of pink print for shell
¼ yard of yellow print for shell
22" outerwear zipper
4 yards of ¼"-diameter cord
1¾ yards of 1½"-wide cotton belting
36" x 45" piece of batting (or scraps)

*If you prefer to cut the shell from a single fabric,
purchase ⅝ yard of quilting cotton.*

ASSEMBLING THE SHELL FABRIC

Cut the assorted prints into squares and rectangles
of various sizes. Sew the pieces together, pressing
the seam allowances to one side as you go, to make
a piece of patchwork at least 23" x 36". Treat the
assembled patchwork as yardage when you cut the
pieces in the following list.

CUTTING

From the pieced fabric, cut:
2 rectangles, 12" x 16½", for sides
2 rectangles, 8½" x 12½", for pockets

From the canvas, cut:
2 rectangles, 12" x 16½", for side interlinings
1 rectangle, 8½" x 30½", for base interlining
2 rectangles, 5½" x 22", for zipper panel interlinings
2 rectangles, 8½" x 12½", for pocket interlinings

*Roomy pockets provide lots of space for stuff—as well as a
canvas for your creativity. A cross-bag strap gives this duffel
easy-wearing flair.*

From the brown-print flannel, cut:
2 rectangles, 12" x 16½", for side linings
1 rectangle, 8½" x 30½", for base lining
2 rectangles, 5½" x 22", for zipper-panel linings
2 rectangles, 8½" x 12½", for pocket linings

From the pink print, cut:
2 rectangles, 5½" x 14½", for zipper panel

From the yellow print, cut:
4 rectangles, 5½" x 4¼", for zipper panel

From the tan print, cut:
1 rectangle, 8½" x 30½", for base
1½"-wide bias strips totaling at least 140" when sewn
    together, for piping

From the belting, cut:
1 piece, 60" long, for strap

From the batting, cut:
2 rectangles, 12" x 16½", for sides
1 rectangle, 8½" x 30½", for base
2 rectangles, 5½" x 22", for zipper panels
2 rectangles, 8½" x 12½", for pockets

Beyond playtime camping gear, the duffel bag also doubles as a great sleepover carryall.

DUFFEL SHELL

1 Create a quilt sandwich from one canvas side rectangle, a corresponding batting rectangle, and one pieced side rectangle. Quilt the layers with straight lines of stitching placed horizontally (parallel to the 16½" edges) and ½" apart. Repeat to quilt the second set of side pieces and the two pockets.

2 Using the tan bias strips and the ¼"-diameter cord, prepare piping as directed in "Piping" on page 13.

3 Baste the prepared piping to one 12½" edge of a quilted pocket, positioning the existing stitches on the piping ⅝" from the fabric raw edges and stitching on top of the previous stitches. This will be the top of the pocket. Layer the quilted pocket and one pocket lining with right sides together, sandwiching the piping between the layers. Sew together with a ⅝" seam. Turn the pocket right side out and align the fabric raw edges at the sides and bottom. Topstitch in the ditch next to the piping. Make two.

4 Lay a pocket, right side up, on a quilted side piece, matching the raw edges on the right and bottom. Pin or clip the pieces together. Make a template from the pattern on page 48. Position the template on the side/pocket unit and trace the curved edge to round one corner. Cut along the traced curve. Round the other three corners, shifting the template as necessary. Make two side units.

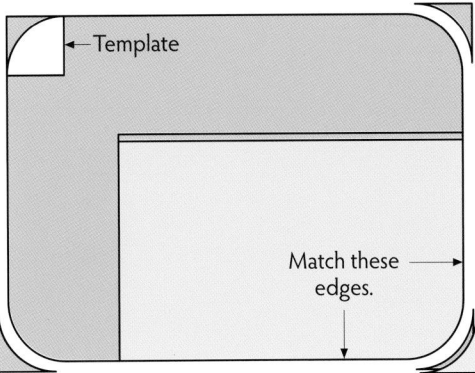

5 Position one end of the strap on a side unit, right sides up, with the strap raw edge at the bottom of the pocket and the strap centered over the pocket raw edge. Edgestitch the strap to the side unit, going up

one edge, across the strap 1½" below the top of the side unit, and then back down the other long edge. Stitch a 1½"-long X at the top of the stitched strap area for reinforcement.

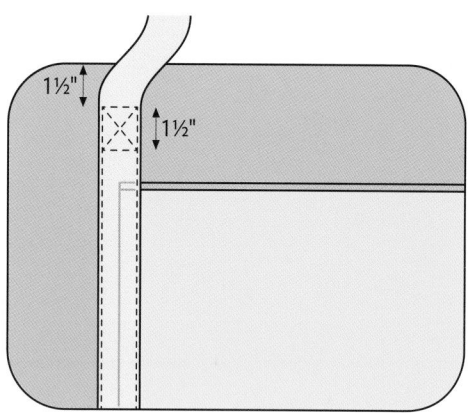

6 Lay the second side unit beside the first with their top edges abutting. Position the free end of the strap on the second side unit, taking care to avoid twists in the strap. Stitch the strap to the second side unit as in step 5.

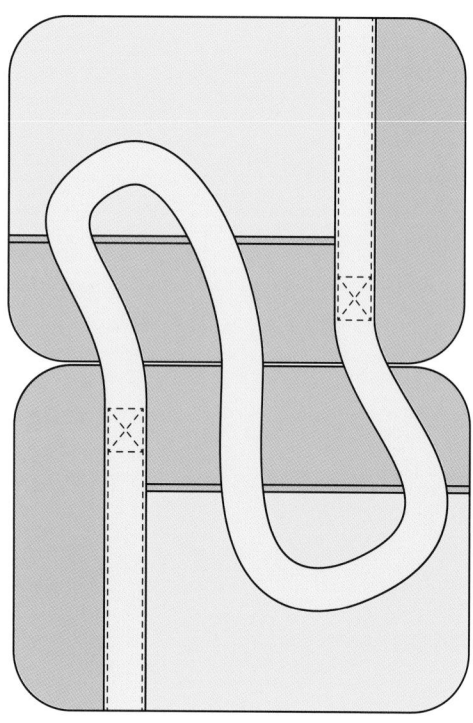

7 Baste piping to the outer edge of each side unit, starting and stopping at the point shown. The piping will be on top of the strap at the bottom edges, but be sure to keep the strap free of the piping at the

top edges. Position the piping's seamline ⅝" from the edges of the side units, and sew directly on top of the previous stitches.

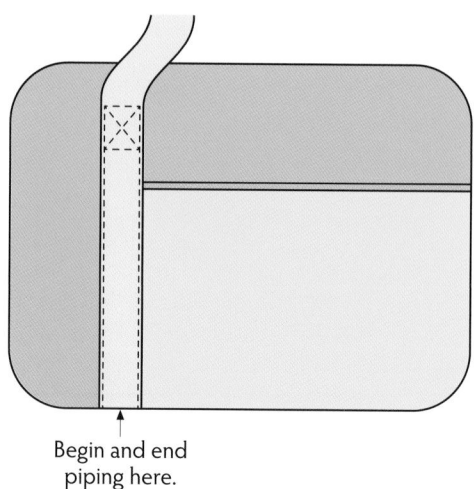

Begin and end piping here.

DUFFEL ZIPPER

1 To make the zipper panels, sew a yellow rectangle to each end of a pink rectangle. Layer the pieced unit with batting and canvas to make a quilt sandwich. Quilt the layers with straight lines of stitching ½" apart, sewing parallel to the short ends of the panel. Make two.

2 Refer to "Zipper Installation" on page 14. For this project, the zipper is the same length as the panels, so there are no tabs at the end. The lining will be attached later, so you'll be working with only the quilted panels now. Sew the zipper to the panels and edgestitch on each side of the zipper.

3 Using the pattern on pages 48–49, make a template for shaping the zipper panel. Begin with a long piece of paper folded across the center to make a complete, 22"-long template. Center the template on the assembled zipper panel, trace the curved edges, and trim along the curves.

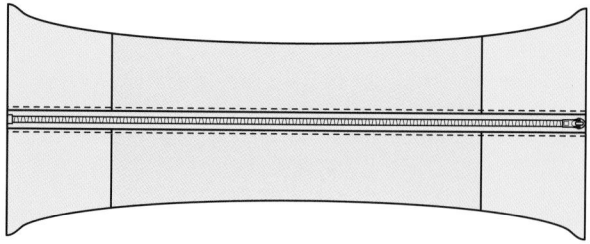

Duffel pockets add the perfect amount of storage.

4 Layer the base rectangle with batting and canvas and quilt as in step 1. Place the base on the zipper panel, right sides together, and sew the short ends using a ⅝" seam allowance to make a ring. Press the seam allowances toward the base and edgestitch the seams.

Zippy Tip

An outerwear zipper with molded plastic or metal teeth works especially well for this project. However, you'll need to be very careful when sewing across the zipper teeth and you may want to end your seam at both sides of the zipper, leaving a ¼" gap in the seam that won't affect the project. You can also use pliers to remove one or two teeth on each side of the zipper, creating a gap for the seam.

5 Fold the assembled base/zipper unit in half, matching the seams, and mark the folds on each edge. These are the top and bottom centers. Refold the gusset, matching the top and bottom marks, and mark the new folds; these are the centers of the side edges. Fold each of the side units in half in both directions and mark the centers.

6 Open the zipper halfway to prepare for turning. Pin the base/zipper unit to the side units, matching the center marks. Continue pinning around the edges, easing the base/zipper unit to fit at the rounded corners and keeping the loose portion of the strap tucked inside the bag. Sew each side to the gusset with a ⅝" seam allowance. Turn the bag right side out.

DUFFEL LINING

1 Use the template from page 48 to round the corners of each lining side. Use the template from pages 48 and 49 to shape one long edge of each zipper panel lining. Press ½" to the wrong side on the remaining straight long edge of each zipper panel lining.

2 Pin the zipper panel lining pieces to the base lining, right sides together, with the pressed edges toward the center of the seam. There should be a ½" gap between the pressed edges. Sew the base to the zipper panels with a ⅝" seam allowance to make the gusset lining. Press the seam allowances toward the base and edgestitch the seams.

3 Mark and sew the lining sides to the gusset as you did for the quilted outer pieces, using ⅝" seam allowances.

FINISHING THE DUFFEL BAG

1 Turn the bag right side out; leave the lining wrong side out. Slip the lining inside the quilted bag and whipstitch the pressed lining edges to the wrong side of the quilted zipper panel.

2 Tack the lining to the shell with a few invisible hand stitches at each upper corner to keep the lining in place.

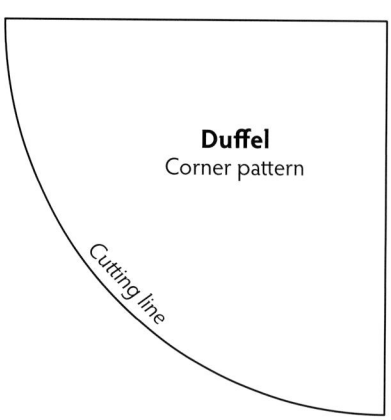

Duffel
Corner pattern

Cutting line

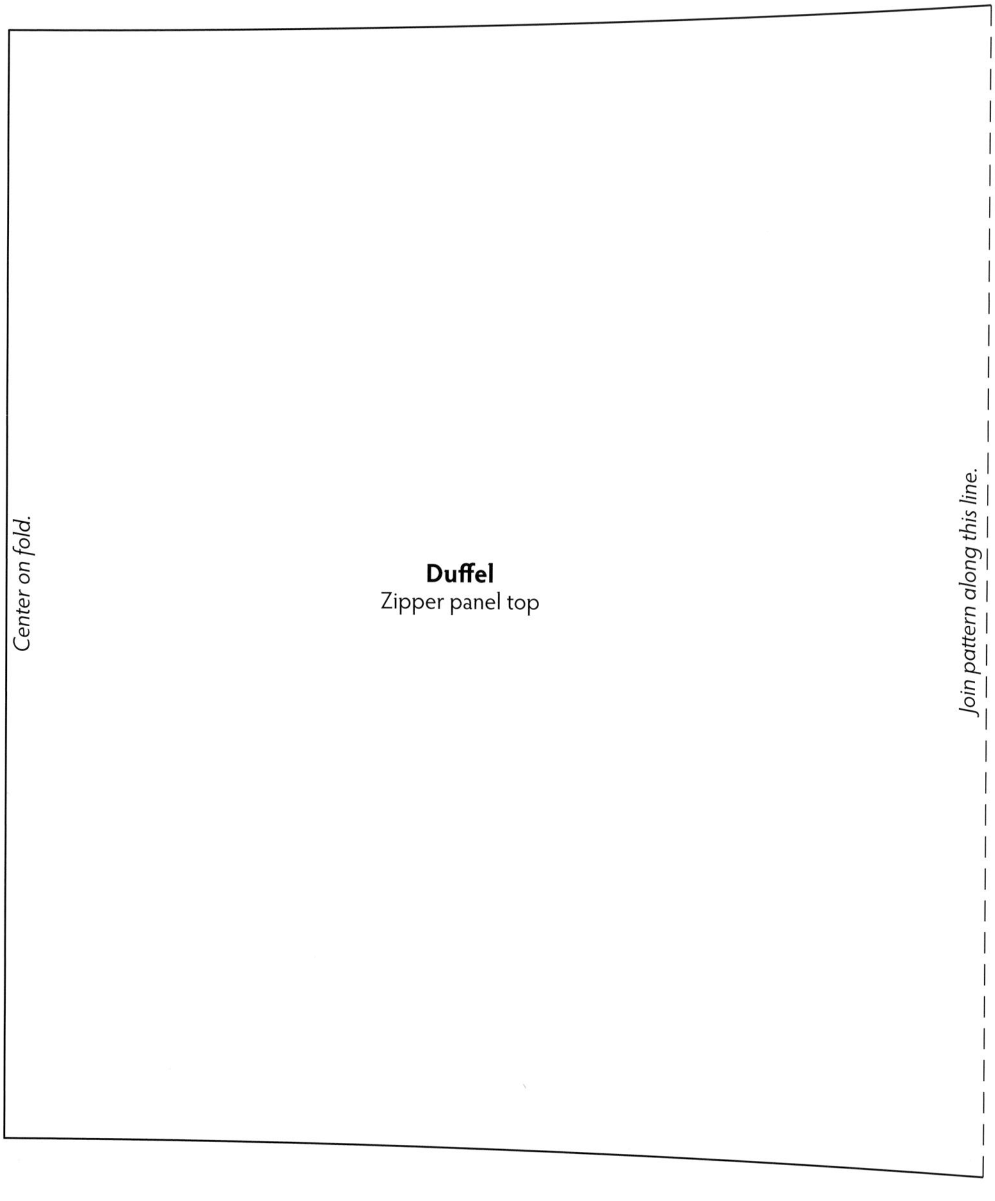

Duffel
Zipper panel top

Center on fold.

Join pattern along this line.

Join pattern along this line.

Duffel
Zipper panel bottom

BINDLE

FINISHED SIZE: 20½" x 20½" open, without stick

MATERIALS

Yardage is based on 42"-wide fabric.

⅔ yard of brown-print flannel for bindle
6 yards of ½"-diameter cord for rope
36" wooden dowel, 1" diameter

CUTTING

From the brown-print flannel, cut:
2 squares, 21" x 21"*

From the cord, cut:
3 pieces, 72" long

*If your fabric is less than 42" wide, decrease the square dimensions to fit the fabric.

BRAIDED ROPE

Braid the three lengths of cord to create a rope. Stitch across the cord 2" from each end to secure the braid, and let the loose ends ravel to create tassels.

Tie the bindle to a stick, and your little one's prized possessions can be carried on great adventures.

MAKING THE BINDLE

1 With right sides together, sew the two flannel squares together, leaving a small gap along one side for turning.

2 Clip the corners diagonally to reduce bulk. Turn the bindle right side out, smoothing the corners into place.

3 Press the bindle, turning the seam allowances to the inside along the gap. Topstitch ⅛" from the edge around all four sides, closing the gap as you stitch.

FINISHING THE BINDLE

Tie the bindle square around the dowel and secure it with the braided rope.

TENT

FINISHED SIZE: 50" wide x 59" long x 36" high

MATERIALS

Yardage is based on 42"-wide fabric unless otherwise noted.

4⅜ yards of 60"-wide natural canvas for tent
1⅜ yards of 54"-wide (or wider) tulle netting for curtains
1⅜ yards of brown print for binding
½ yard of brown-print flannel for curtain ties
Scraps of miscellaneous trims, 13" to 16" long
Assorted large buttons
5¼ yards of ¾"-wide Velcro
¾"-diameter PVC pipes and fittings
- 6 pipes, 30" long
- 4 pipes, 40" long
- 4 couplings
- 4 elbows, 90°
- 2 tees, 90°

The play-sized tent is perfect for indoor campouts.

CUTTING

From the canvas, cut:
2 squares, 60" x 60", for tent sides
1 rectangle, 20" x 60", for tent floor
1 square, 10" x 10", for tent awning

From the brown-print flannel, cut:
4 rectangles, 6½" x 12", for curtain ties

From the netting, cut:
1 square, 45" x 45", for curtains

From the brown print, cut:
1½"-wide bias strips totaling at least 512" when sewn together, for single-fold binding
2½"-wide bias strips totaling at least 190" when sewn together, for double-fold binding

From the Velcro, cut:
4 pieces, 45" long
4 pieces, 1½" long

MAKING THE TENT

1 Join the sides along one edge with a topstitched French seam, referring to "Topstitched French Seams" on page 13. This will be the top of the tent.

2 Sew the floor panel to the opposite edge of one side with a topstitched French seam. Sew the

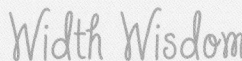

Width Wisdom

Sometimes a fabric marketed as 60" wide doesn't quite measure up. If you find that your canvas is a little narrow, you can increase the width to 60" by piecing or, if the difference is small, by making a wider binding. It's important that the tent panels measure a full 60" when finished so that they will fit the PVC pipe frame. Alternatively, trim the pipes to fit the narrower fabric of your tent.

opposite edge of the floor to the bottom of the second side panel with a topstitched French seam, making a ring of fabric.

3 Referring to "Single-Fold Binding" on page 10, assemble the brown 1½"-wide bias strips to make binding. Cut the 10" awning square in half diagonally from corner to corner. Bind the longest side of each triangle.

4 Sew a prepared awning triangle between the two side panels at the top front of the tent as shown in the photographs. Sew the pieces with right sides together. Repeat to stitch the second triangle to the top back of the tent.

5 Bind the front and back edges of the tent. Continue the binding across the floor panels, and include the awning seam allowances in the binding. The awnings will fold forward, covering the binding, when the tent is complete.

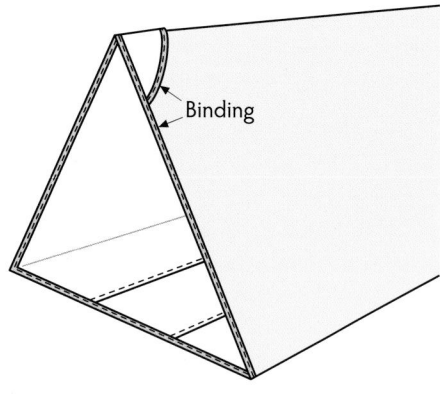

Binding

6 Separate the halves of the 45"-long Velcro pieces. Sew one piece of the hook tape to the inside surface of each tent side panel, ¼" from the binding, beginning at the top seam. Be sure the awnings are folded out of the way.

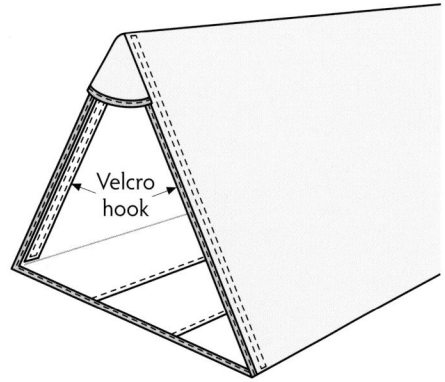

Velcro hook

MAKING THE CURTAINS

1 Following the instructions in "Double-Fold Binding" on page 12, assemble the brown 2½"-wide bias strips to make binding. Cut the 45" netting square in half diagonally from corner to corner to create two triangles, and bind the 45" sides of each triangle. Position a strip of the Velcro loop on the right side of each curtain, ¼" from each bound edge, beginning at the angle between the 45" sides.

2 Use the single-fold binding prepared in step 1 of "Making the Tent" to bind the long edge of each triangle. This will be the bottom edge of the curtain. Use the Velcro strips to hang one curtain in the back opening of the tent.

3 Fold the remaining curtain in half from the longest edge to the opposite corner and cut along the fold. Use the single-fold binding to finish each of the newly cut edges. These two triangles will be the front curtains.

MAKING THE TIES

1 The ties are made like binding, so refer to "Single-Fold Binding" on page 10 for details. After pressing, temporarily unfold each tie and press ¼" to the wrong side on both ends. Refold, press, and topstitch ⅛" from all four edges of the tie. Make four.

2 Separate the halves of the 1½"-long Velcro pieces. Position a hook section on one side of a tie, aligning it with one end. Position a loop section on the reverse side of the same tie, immediately behind the hook tape. Edgestitch through all layers. Repeat for the remaining three ties.

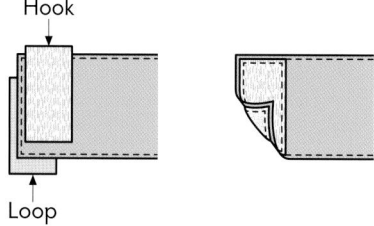

Hook

Loop

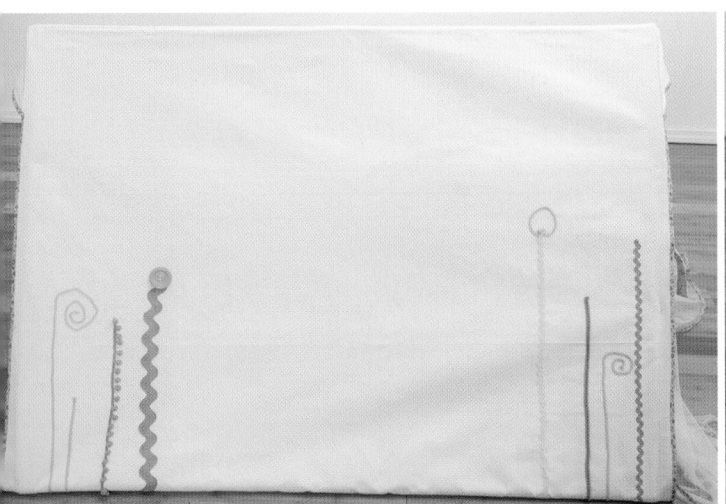

Ribbons, rick-rack, and novelty trims paired with buttons add a touch of whimsy to the tent exterior.

3 Attach two ties to the Velcro strip on one side of the front tent opening, placing the ties one on top of the other. Position the other two ties on the opposite side of the front opening. Attach one of the front curtains to each side, using the Velcro on both the tent and the ties to hold the curtain in place. Wrap and knot the ties around the curtains to hold them open.

The Velcro on the curtain ties fits between the tent and the curtain.

FINISHING THE TENT

1 Stitch the scraps of trim to the sides of the tent as desired to represent stems. Add buttons at the top of each stem to create flowers. Use your imagination to vary the trims, personalizing the tent for your little one.

2 Connect the 30" pipes in pairs to make three tent supports, each 60" long. Use a T joint to connect two 40" pipes to one end of one tent support; repeat at the other end of the same 60" pipe unit.

3 Working inside the canvas tent, place an elbow on the free end of each 40" pipe and use them to connect the other two tent supports to the frame. Notice that the seams connecting the floor to the side panels do not lie along the pipes.

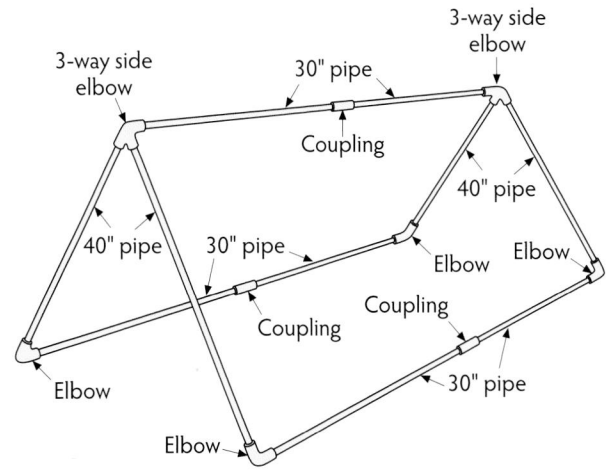

KITCHEN COOKING

An apron, oven mitt, hot pads, and a tablecloth are the essential ingredients for a pretend kitchen. These projects will get things cookin' in the little kitchen. Consider using the tablecloth as practical mess-protection when a little one is crafting.

TASTY KITCHEN APRON

Finished size: 11¾" x 18" without ties

MATERIALS

Yardage is based on 42"-wide fabric.

½ yard of red print for apron body
⅜ yard of pink print for ties
½ yard of yellow-green solid for binding
¼ yard of multicolored print for pocket
1 yard of ⅜"-wide lace edging

CUTTING

From the red print, cut:
1 rectangle, 9" x 42", for apron body
1 rectangle, 6½" x 18½", for waistband

From the multicolored print, cut:
1 rectangle, 5½" x 11", for pocket

From the pink print, cut:
2 rectangles, 5½" x 30", for ties

From the yellow-green solid, cut:
1½"-wide bias strips totaling at least 120"
when sewn together, for binding

APRON FRONT

1 Use the yellow-green bias strips to prepare the binding, referring to "Single-Fold Binding" on page 10.

2 Make a template from the corner pattern on page 57. Position the template on an upper corner of the pocket, trace around the curved edge, and cut along the curve to round the corner. Repeat to round the second upper corner of the pocket rectangle. Bind the sides and top edge of the pocket. Lay the lace trim over the binding and topstitch it into place.

3 Decide which 42" edge of the apron body will be the lower edge. Use the corner template to round the two bottom corners. Fold and finger-press the pocket and apron body in half to find their vertical

Gathers and a fancy pocket give this little apron a big helping of style.

centerlines. Lay the pocket on the apron body, right sides up, matching the centers and lower edge. Topstitch along the centerline, backstitching at the ends to secure the seam. Measure 5" from the bottom of the apron along the sides of the pocket and mark. Topstitch along the binding stitches from the bottom of the apron to each mark, backstitching at the ends of the seams.

4 Gather the top of the apron, referring to "Ruffle" on page 15. Pull the threads and adjust the top of the apron to measure 18½".

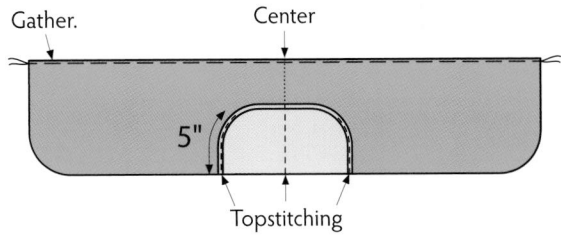

Gather.   Center

5"

Topstitching

Good Gathering

As you adjust the gathers, keep about ½" flat at each side of the apron. This gather-free space will make apron assembly a bit easier.

Contrasting binding adds a retro flair to the apron edge.

5 Fold the waistband in half lengthwise with wrong sides together and press. Lay the waistband on the wrong side of the apron, aligning the raw edges. Distribute the gathers evenly along the waistband and pin. Stitch the waistband seam and press the seam allowances toward the waistband.

6 Position a strip of prepared bias binding over the seam on the apron right side, covering the seam allowances, and bind the seam. Trim the raw edges if necessary so that they will be completely concealed by the bias trim. Turn the bound seam toward the waistband and edgestitch the free edge of the binding to the waistband.

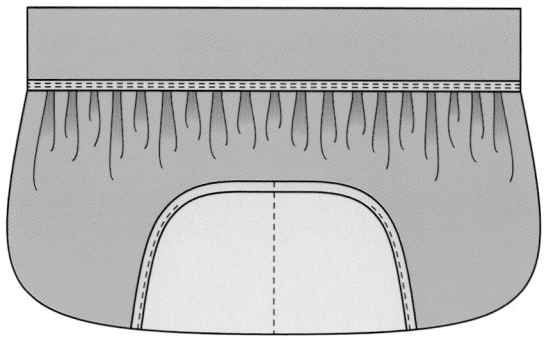

TIES

1 Fold a tie rectangle in half lengthwise with right sides together. Mark one short end of the folded tie at a 45° angle from the fold to the raw edges, creating a point. Cut along the angled line. Sew the long edge and angled end, leaving the short straight edge open for turning. Make two.

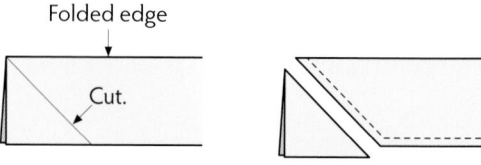

2 Trim the corners diagonally to reduce bulk. Turn the ties right side out and press, smoothing the corners into place. Topstitch ¼" from the seamlines and folded edge.

3 On the open end of a tie, measure and mark 1" from the folded edge and ½" from the stitched long edge. Fold the tie along the 1" mark and bring the fold to meet the ½" mark, forming a pleat. Baste ⅛" from the raw edges to secure the pleat. Repeat for the second tie.

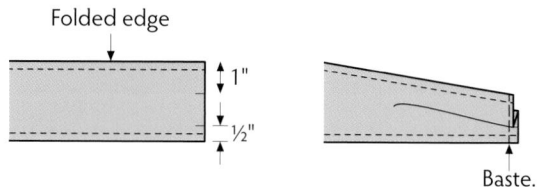

4 Pin the raw edge of a tie to each side of the waistband. The ties should lie on the wrong side of the waistband, with their folded edges aligned. Sew the ties to the waistband ends.

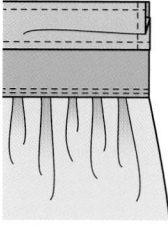

Make It Simple

Skip the Velcro on the Task Apron (page 31) to make a less frilly kitchen apron.

FINISHING THE APRON

1 Bind the side and bottom edges of the apron, enclosing the raw edges of the tie in the binding. Begin and end the binding by turning under ¼" of binding to create clean edges at the top of the waistband.

2 Turn the ties outward, away from the waistband, and topstitch through the binding to hold the ties in position.

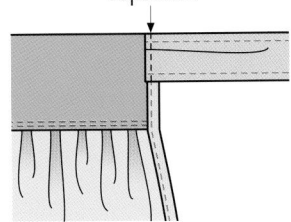

Topstitch.

3 Make a bow from the leftover lace trim and tack it to the pocket with a few hand stitches.

Tasty Kitchen Apron corner pattern
Tablecloth corner pattern
Diaper Bag corner pattern
Changing Pad corner pattern
Receiving Blanket corner pattern
Critter Carrier corner pattern

Cutting line

Imagine the fun little ones will have whipping up pretend treats using their pint-size kitchen collection.

TABLECLOTH

FINISHED SIZE: 36" x 36"

MATERIALS

Yardage is based on 42"-wide fabric.

1⅛ yards *each* of multicolored polka dot and red print for tablecloth

CUTTING

From *each* fabric, cut:
1 square, 36" x 36"

MAKING THE TABLECLOTH

1 Place the two fabric squares right sides together with raw edges matched.

2 Use the pattern on page 57 to make a template for rounding the corners. Position the template on a corner of the stacked fabrics, trace the curved edge, and cut along the curved line. Repeat to round all four corners.

3 Sew around all four edges, leaving a gap along one side for turning. Notch the corner curves to reduce bulk, and turn the tablecloth right side out.

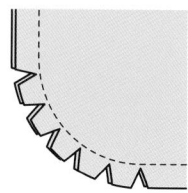

FINISHING THE TABLECLOTH

1 Press the tablecloth edges, turning the seam allowances to the inside along the opening.

2 Topstitch ⅛" from the edge around the entire tablecloth, closing the opening as you sew.

Made with two equally charming prints, this quick and simple tablecloth is always ready to be of service.

OVEN MITT AND HOT PADS

FINISHED SIZES: Oven mitt: 6¼" x 9",
Hot pads: 6½" x 6½"

MATERIALS

Yardage is based on 42"-wide fabric and makes 1 oven mitt and 2 hot pads.

¼ yard of pink print for oven mitt
¼ yard of paisley print for oven mitt
¼ yard of multicolored polka dot for hot pads
¼ yard of red print for hot pads
¼ yard of yellow-green solid for binding
½ yard of heat-resistant batting
¼ yard of pink rickrack

Scrap Sense

The materials listed here will be plenty to make at least one oven mitt and two hot pads as shown. If you prefer, use scraps from other projects to create these little accessories.

CUTTING

Trace the oven mitt pattern on page 61 onto plain paper to make a template.

From the pink print, cut:
2 oven mitts

From the paisley print, cut:
2 oven mitts, reversed

From the multicolored polka dot, cut:
2 squares, 6½" x 6½", for hot pad

From the red print, cut:
2 squares, 6½" x 6½", for hot pad

Heat-resistant batting makes these oven mitts and hot pads functional as well as fun.

From the yellow-green solid, cut:
1½"-wide bias strips totaling at least 60" when sewn together, for binding

From the batting, cut:
2 oven mitts
2 squares, 6½" x 6½"

Easy Reversal

To cut the reversed pieces for the oven mitt, you can turn the template wrong side up when placing it on the fabric. For a quick alternative, just stack the two pieces of fabric with wrong sides together and cut as one; as you cut each pair of pieces, you'll automatically reverse one. For the sample oven mitt shown, the pink print is right side up on top of the stack, and both pairs of pieces are cut with the template right side up. The result is an oven mitt with different fabrics on its front and back surfaces.

Kids will love baking up make-believe fun with these sassy kitchen accessories.

MAKING THE OVEN MITT

1 Layer two coordinating fabric pieces with batting sandwiched between them. Match the raw edges, and remember, as you plan for the inner and outer surfaces, that one sandwich will be reversed. Quilt each piece with straight horizontal lines ½" apart. Trim the edges to neaten them, if necessary.

2 Place the two quilted oven mitts right sides together and sew, leaving the straight edge open. Trim the seam allowance to ⅛" and overcast with a zigzag stitch if desired. Turn the mitt right side out.

3 Use the yellow-green bias strips to prepare the binding, referring to "Single-Fold Binding" on page 10. Bind the straight edge of the mitt, beginning at the side opposite the thumb. When you return to the starting point, angle the bias binding off the edge and continue sewing the edges of the bias binding together for 4½". As you near the 4½" point, stop sewing and cut the bias ¼" beyond the end point. Unfold the end of the bias, finger-press the raw edge to the wrong side, and refold the binding before finishing the seam.

4 Fold the trailing loop of binding in half, bringing the loose end to overlap the straight edge of the oven mitt. Position the binding end inside the mitt at the point where the binding angles away from the edge. Sew the end to the oven mitt.

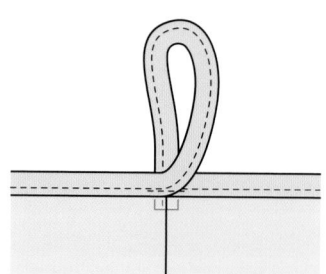

MAKING THE HOT PADS

1 Stack the two cotton squares and the batting square to make a quilt sandwich. Quilt with straight horizontal lines ½" apart.

2 Lay a piece of rickrack across the hot pad, 2" below the upper edge. Topstitch through the center of the rickrack to secure it to the hot pad. Trim the excess rickrack at the sides.

3 Follow the instructions in steps 3 and 4 of "Making the Oven Mitt" to bind the edges of the hot pad. Begin the binding at one corner and make the loop there. Miter the other three corners as you come to them. Repeat to make a second hot pad.

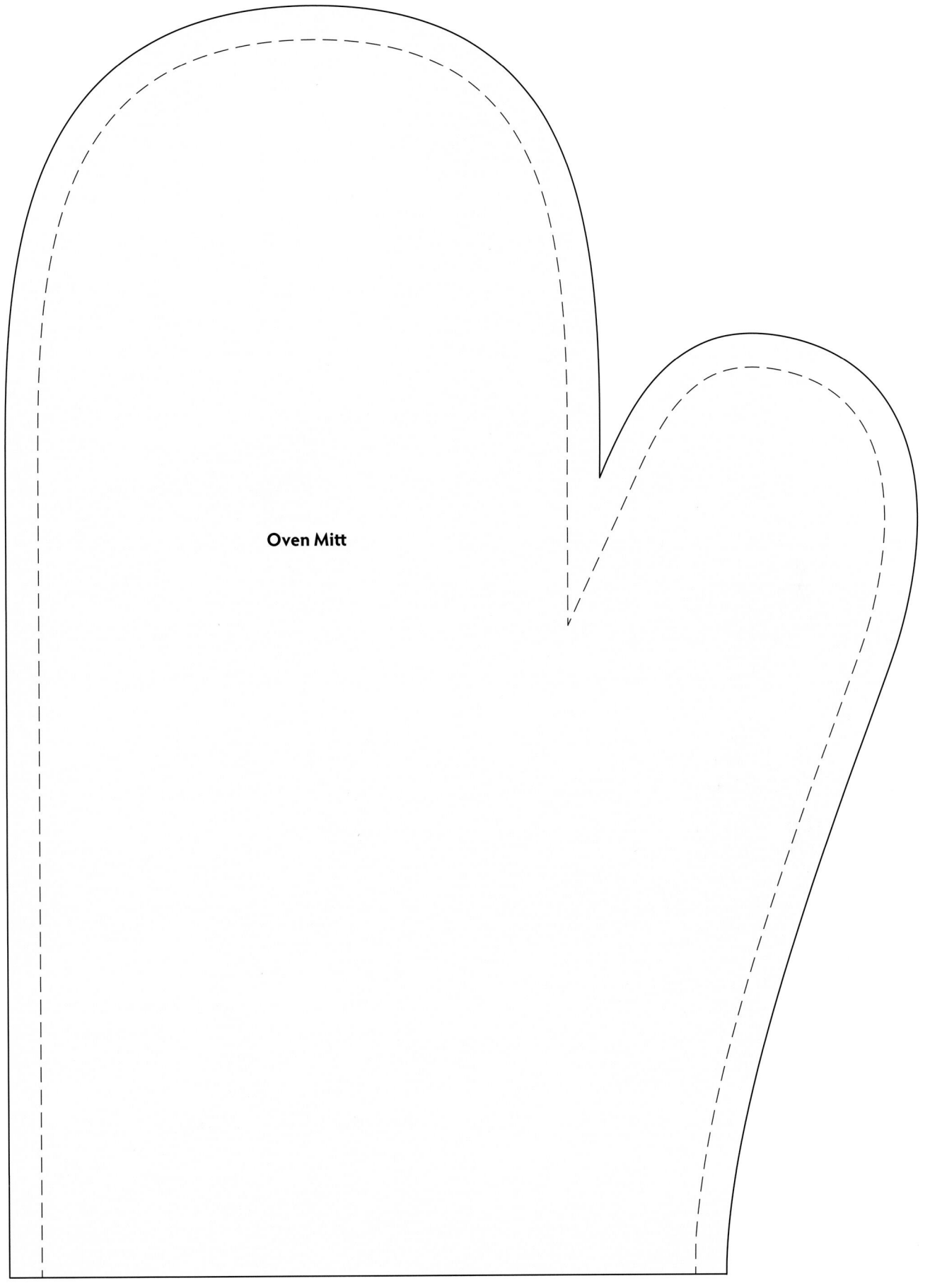

Oven Mitt

BABY LOVE

All the items in the Baby Love collection were created with a little one's tender loving heart and plenty of doll-focused play in mind, but they definitely can be repurposed. You might use the diaper bag as a purse or satchel, or change the dimensions of the blanket to make a wonderful travel blanket for all ages.

DIAPER BAG AND CHANGING PAD

FINISHED SIZES: Diaper bag: 9" wide x 9½" high x 2½" deep, Changing pad: 11" x 18"

MATERIALS

Yardage is based on 42"-wide fabric unless otherwise noted.

⅞ yard of green print for strap, elastic pocket, ties, and changing pad

⅝ yard of blue print for bag, strap, interior pocket, and changing pad

½ yard of chevron stripe for lining and exterior pocket

⅛ yard of 60"-wide floral-print knit for flower

⅓ yard of ¼"-wide elastic

11" x 18" piece of medium-loft batting

CUTTING

From the blue print, cut:
2 rectangles, 9½" x 10", for bag panels
2 rectangles, 3" x 10", for side panels
1 rectangle, 3" x 9½", for base
1 rectangle, 6½" x 10", for interior pocket
1 rectangle, 2½" x 26", for strap
1 rectangle, 11" x 18", for changing pad

From the green print, cut:
1 rectangle, 12" x 14", for elastic pocket
1 rectangle, 2½" x 26", for strap
1 rectangle, 11" x 18", for changing pad
1½"-wide bias strips totaling at least 130"
    when sewn together, for ties and binding

From the chevron stripe, cut:
2 rectangles, 9½" x 10", for lining panels
2 rectangles, 3" x 10", for lining side panels
1 rectangle, 3" x 9½", for lining base
1 rectangle, 9½" x 12", for exterior pocket

Any doll's parents would be happy to have this set.

PREPARE THE POCKETS

1 Fold the exterior pocket rectangle in half, wrong sides together, matching the 9½" edges. Topstitch ¼" from the folded edge.

2 Lay the pocket on one bag panel, right sides up, matching the side and bottom edges. Measure and mark a vertical line across the pocket 3½" from the right edge. Topstitch along the line, backstitching at the upper edge of the pocket to secure the stitches.

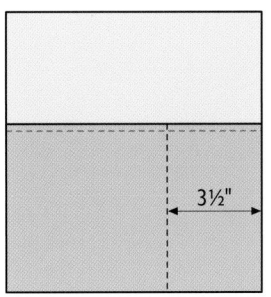

3 Fold the interior-pocket rectangle in half with right sides together, matching the 6½" edges. Sew along the raw edges, leaving a small gap along one edge for turning. Trim the corners diagonally to reduce bulk. Turn the pocket right side out, smoothing the corners into place, and press, turning the seam allowances to the wrong side along the gap. Topstitch ¼" from the folded edge; this is the top of the pocket.

Optional Flap

If you'd like to add a flap, with or without a ruffle, to your diaper bag, follow these additional instructions.

ADDITIONAL MATERIALS

⅜ yard of fabric for flap lining
¼ yard of fabric for flap
¼ yard of fabric for ruffle, zipper tabs,
    and zipper-pocket lining
9" zipper

CUTTING

From the fabric for the flap, cut:
1 rectangle, 5" x 9", for lower flap
1 rectangle, 6" x 9", for upper flap

From the fabric for the flap lining, cut:
1 rectangle, 9" x 10½", for flap lining

From the fabric for the ruffle and tabs, cut:
1 strip, 2" x 40", for ruffle (optional)
1 rectangle, 6" x 9", for zipper-pocket lining
1 rectangle, 5" x 9", for zipper-pocket lining
2 rectangles, 2" x 4", for zipper tabs

MAKING THE OPTIONAL FLAP

1 Prepare the zipper tabs as instructed in "Zipper Installation" on page 14. Install the zipper as directed, using the pocket-lining rectangles as the lining layer. When the zipper installation is complete, fold the longer pocket lining down to match the raw edges at the bottom of the pocket and flap. Pin or clip the layers together.

2 Make a template from the corner pattern on page 57. Position the template on the bottom-right corner of the flap, trace the curved edge, and cut along the traced line.

3 Following the instructions in "Ruffle" on page 15, make the ruffle and attach it to the right and bottom edges of the assembled flap. Where the ruffle ends at the lower-left corner, bring the raw edges at the end of the ruffle down to meet the seamline, tapering the ruffle width to zero at the corner. Baste the ruffle in place.

4 Place the flap lining on the flap assembly, right sides together, with the ruffle sandwiched between the layers. Trim the rounded corner of the lining to match the flap. Sew the layers together along the sides and bottom edge, leaving the short edge at the top of the flap open.

5 Clip the curve and trim the corner diagonally. Turn the flap right side out and press flat. Topstitch ¼" from the sides and bottom edge, keeping the ruffle free of the topstitching.

6 To attach the flap to the diaper bag, baste it to the back bag panel, right sides together, before you attach the lining to the bag.

4 Center the pocket on one lining panel with right sides up. Topstitch ⅛" from the side and bottom edges, backstitching at the top edge and leaving the top edge open. This is the front lining panel.

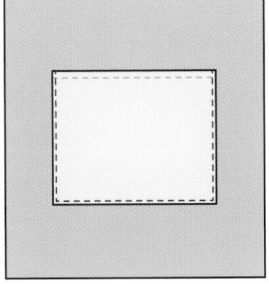

Lining front

5 Fold the elastic pocket in half with wrong sides together, matching the 14" edges. Cut a 9½" length of elastic. Slip the elastic between the layers of the folded pocket, sliding it all the way to the fold. Pin each end of the elastic to the side of the folded pocket. Baste ⅛" from each end of the elastic to hold the ends in place. Topstitch ⅝" from the fold, forming a casing around the elastic; be careful not to catch the elastic in these stitches. Stretch and release the elastic to distribute it evenly along the pocket width.

6 Measure along the bottom edge of the pocket and mark as shown. Fold the pocket, wrong sides together, at the first A mark. Bring the fold to meet the nearest B mark, forming a pleat, and pin at the bottom edge. Repeat to make a total of four pleats along the bottom edge of the pocket. Notice that the pleats nearest the center open toward the center and the outer pleats open toward the sides.

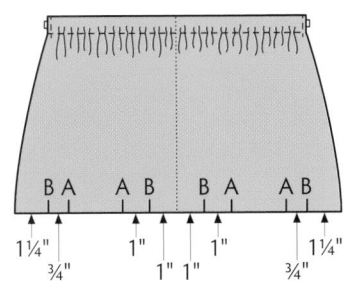

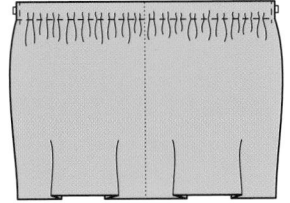

7 Fold both the elastic pocket and the remaining lining panel in half and finger-press along their vertical centerlines. Lay the pocket on the lining panel, right sides up, matching the centerlines, sides, and bottom edge. Adjust the pleats, if necessary, so that the side seams match correctly. Topstitch the pocket to the lining along the centerline, backstitching at the upper edge to secure. Baste ⅛" from the side and bottom edges.

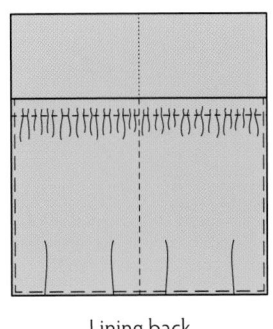

Lining back

BAG BODY AND STRAP

1 Use the green bias strips to prepare the binding, referring to "Single-Fold Binding" on page 10.

2 Cut a 10½"-long piece of the prepared bias binding. Temporarily open one end of the strip, press ¼" of the raw edge to the wrong side, and refold. Edgestitch the long open edge to form a tie. Make four. Position a tie on each side of each body panel, 2½" below the top edge, with right sides together and raw edges matched. Baste ⅛" from the raw edges to hold the ties in place.

3 Layer the strap pieces with right sides together and sew both long edges. Turn the strap right out and press flat. Topstitch ¼" from each long edge.

4 Sew the base to the lower edge of the bag front panel. Sew the back panel to the opposite edge of the base.

5 Stitch a side panel to the bag front, sewing from the top of the bag to the intersection with the base seamline; do not stitch across the seam allowances. Stitch the bag back to the opposite edge of the side panel, again stopping at the base seam. Sew the side

panel to the end of the base, stitching between the base seamlines. Repeat to attach the second side panel to the other side of the bag.

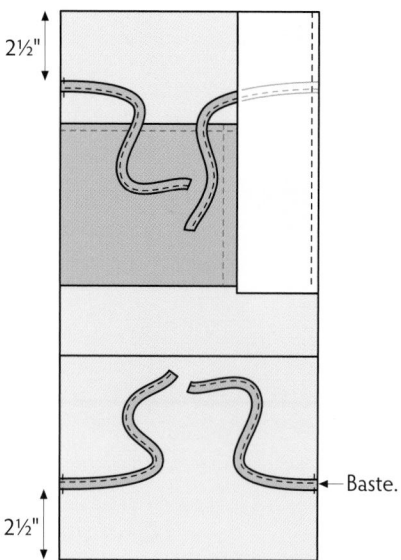

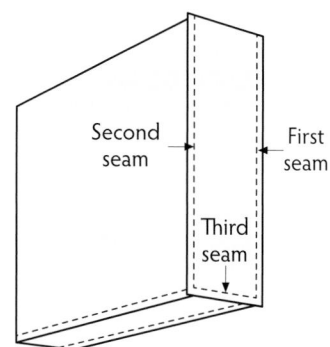

6 Center one end of the strap on the top edge of each side panel, right sides together. Stitch ⅛" from the raw edges to baste the strap to the bag.

LINING

Sew the lining panels together as you did the body panels, leaving a gap in one panel/base seam for turning.

FINISHING THE DIAPER BAG

1 Turn the bag right side out; leave the lining wrong side out. Slip the lining over the bag exterior with right sides together. Position the lining panel with the elastic pocket against the plain exterior panel (the bag back). Be sure the strap and ties are tucked between the layers and out of the way. Stitch the top edge.

2 Turn the project right side out through the gap in the lining seam. Press the top edge and press the seam allowances to the wrong side along the gap in the lining. Topstitch ¼" from the upper edge.

3 Close the gap in the lining by matching the pressed edges and edgestitching, or use hand-sewn whipstitches.

MAKING THE FLOWER

1 Make a template from the largest circle pattern on page 67. Use it to cut seven circles from the knit fabric.

2 Fold one circle in half, wrong sides together, and then in thirds. Trim the outer edge slightly to make a petal shape. Repeat to make six folded petals.

3 Pin the folded petals to the remaining circle. The petal points should meet at the center of the flower.

4 Make templates from the small and medium circle patterns on page 67. Center the smallest template on the flower and trace around it; topstitch along the line. Repeat with the second template to make a second topstitched circle, securing the petals to the base.

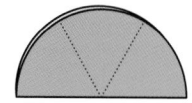 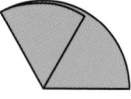 

Make 6.

Trim folded petals.

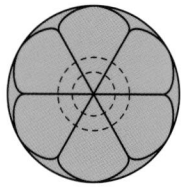

5 Trim the base layer where it extends beyond the petal edges. Hand or machine sew the flower to the pocket of the diaper bag, using the photo as a guide.

CHANGING PAD

1 Draw lines across one changing pad rectangle 6" from each 11" edge. Make a quilt sandwich of the unmarked rectangle, wrong side up; the batting; and the marked rectangle, right side up. Quilt on the marked lines through all the layers.

2 Make a template from the pattern on page 57. Position the template on one corner of the changing pad, trace the curved edge, and cut along the line to round the corner. Repeat to round all four corners.

3 Cut a piece of bias binding 11" long. Temporarily open one end, press ¼" to the wrong side, and refold. Stitch the long open edges and the pressed end to make a tie. Make two.

4 Fold the pad in half to find the centers of the long edges and mark. Position one tie on the right side of the pad at each mark, matching the raw edges, with the bulk of the ties toward the center of the pad. Baste ⅛" from the raw edges.

Hours of fun are sure to be had with this realistic set.

Baste.

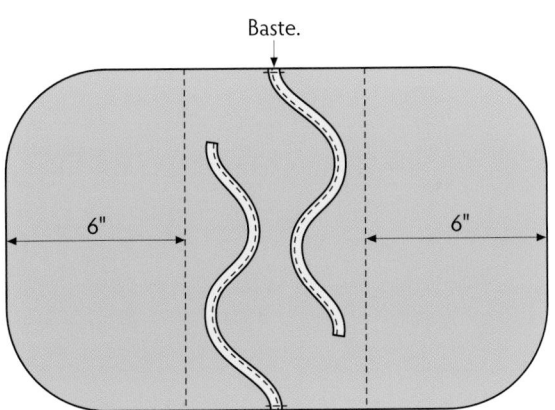

6"   6"

5 Referring to "Single-Fold Binding" on page 10, bind the edge of the changing pad.

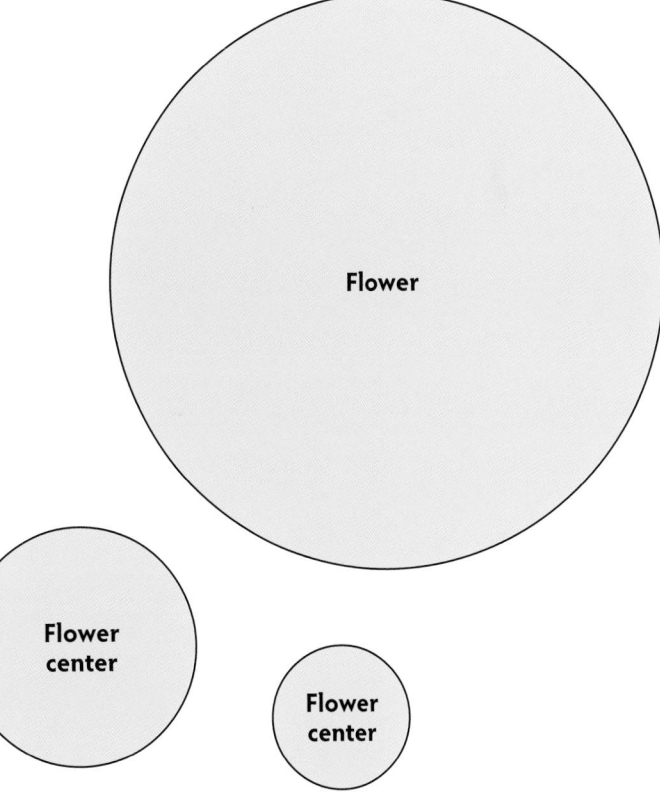

Flower

Flower center

Flower center

RECEIVING BLANKET, BURP CLOTH, AND SLING

FINISHED SIZES: Receiving Blanket: 20" x 26",
Burp Cloth: 6" x 9¾", Sling: 10" x 19"

MATERIALS

Yardage is based on 60"-wide knit fabric.

1⅛ yards of pink floral knit*

*If you prefer to make the blanket from a different, complementary fabric, you'll need ⅝ yard of white floral for the blanket and ½ yard of pink floral for the remaining items.

CUTTING

From the knit fabric, cut:
1 rectangle, 20" x 26", for receiving blanket
1 rectangle, 10" x 40", for sling
1 burp cloth from the pattern on page 69
4 strips, 1½" x 60", for binding

Cutting Notes

Cut each piece except the burp cloth with its long dimension running across the fabric from selvage to selvage to take advantage of the knit's stretch.

Cut the binding strips last; if you are short on fabric, the binding can be pieced from shorter (less than 60") strips.

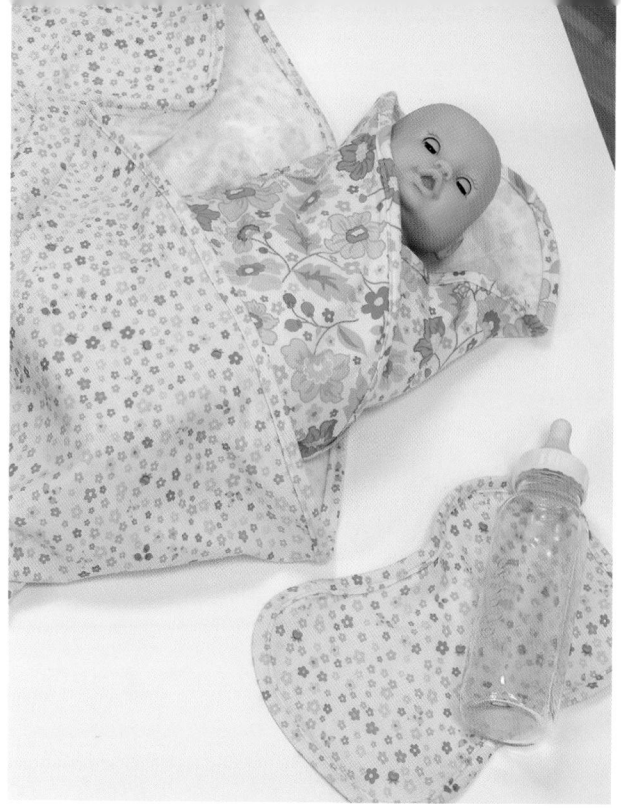

Accessories make caring for Dolly a piece of cake. Swaddle and burp the doll, then carry her everywhere you want to go.

MAKING THE PROJECTS

1 Use the 1½"-wide strips of knit fabric to prepare the binding, referring to "Single-Fold Binding" on page 10.

2 Make a template from the corner pattern on page 57. Position the template on one corner of the 20" x 26" rectangle, trace the curved edge, and trim along the curve. Repeat to round the other three corners.

3 Bind the edges of the receiving blanket and burp cloth.

4 Join the 10" ends of the sling with a topstitched French seam, referring to "Topstitched French Seams" on page 13.

5 Bind the two raw edges of the sling.

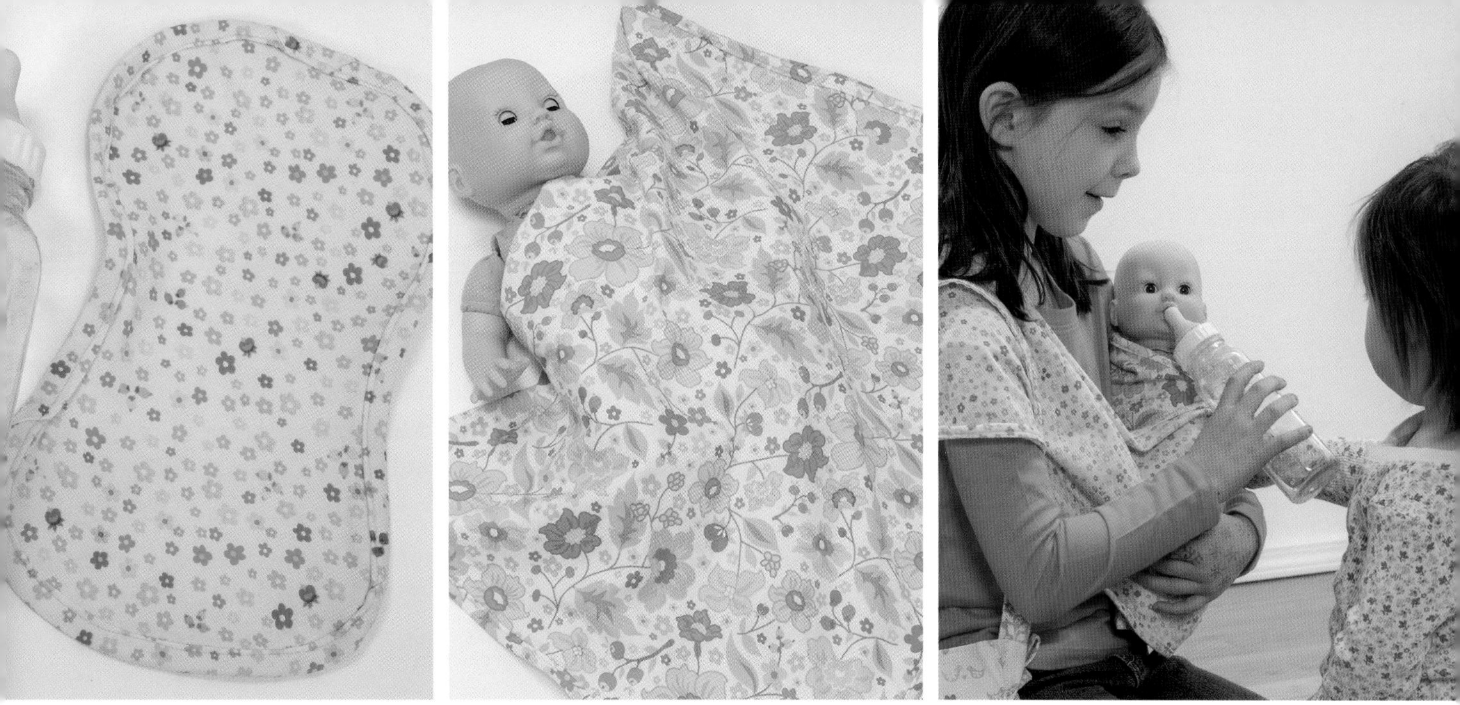

Doll-care accessories make playtime even more precious.

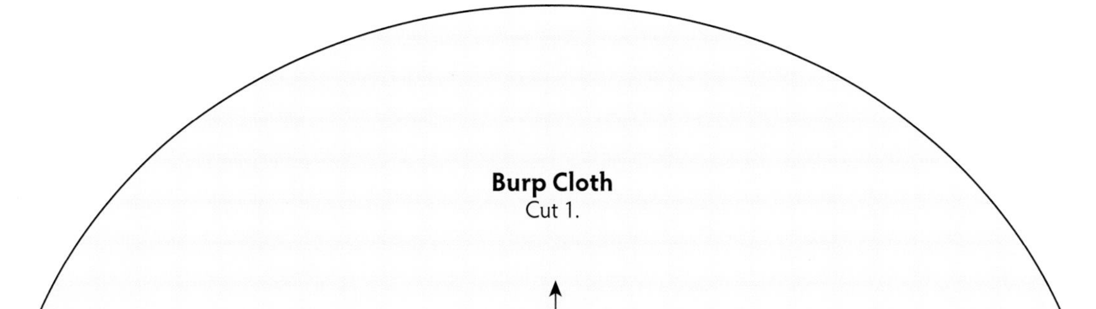

Burp Cloth
Cut 1.

Straight of grain

Flip on dashed line to complete pattern .

PET PRACTICE

Although the pet carrier, bed, and leash were created for a little one's toy-based pet play, they could be repurposed: the carrier could become an adventure tote, and the pillow, enlarged, could transform into a real pet's—or child's—lounge pad.

CRITTER CARRIER

Finished size: 10½" wide x 7½" high x 5½" deep

The pint-sized critter carrier features pet-screen windows and a lowered panel so the stuffed friend's head can poke through for a better view.

MATERIALS

Yardage is based on 42"-wide fabric unless otherwise noted. A fat quarter measures 18" x 21".

⅜ yard of dark-brown print for flaps, sides, base, and straps

⅜ yard of turquoise print for straps, bag, and interior pocket

¼ yard of multicolored dot for flap linings

¼ yard of light-blue print for lining base

¼ yard of pet-themed print for bag

¼ yard of blue stripe for lining

1 fat quarter of green pindot for binding

⅜ yard of 58"-wide padded stabilizer (ByAnnie's Soft and Stable)

6" x 8" piece of pet screening

2½" length of ¾"-wide Velcro

1 yard of 1"-wide cotton webbing

CUTTING

From the turquoise print, cut:
2 rectangles, 4" x 11", for bag front and back
1 rectangle, 6" x 10", for interior pocket
2 rectangles, 2" x 18", for strap linings

From the pet-themed print, cut:
2 rectangles, 4½" x 11", for bag front and back

From the dark-brown print, cut:
1 rectangle, 6" x 8", for long side
1 square, 6" x 6", for short side
1 rectangle, 6" x 11", for base
2 rectangles, 5" x 10½", for flaps
2 rectangles, 2" x 18", for straps

From the multicolored dot, cut:
2 rectangles, 5" x 10½", for flap linings

From the light-blue print, cut:
1 rectangle, 6" x 11", for base lining

From the blue stripe, cut:
2 rectangles, 8" x 11", for lining front and back
1 rectangle, 6" x 8", for long side
1 square, 6" x 6", for short side

From the green pindot, cut:
1½"-wide bias strips totaling at least 80" after joining, for binding

From the padded stabilizer, cut:
2 rectangles, 8" x 11", for front and back
1 rectangle, 6" x 8", for long side
1 square, 6" x 6", for short side
1 rectangle, 6" x 11", for base
2 rectangles, 5" x 10½", for flaps

From the webbing, cut:
2 pieces, 18" long

CRITTER CARRIER SIDES

1 Sew a turquoise 4" x 11" rectangle to the top edge of each pet-print rectangle. Press the seam allowances toward the pet print.

2 Layer a corresponding stabilizer rectangle on the wrong side of each assembled panel. Baste ⅛" from the edges.

3 Using the window pattern on page 74, create a template for the carrier windows. Center the template on one assembled panel, 1¼" below the top edge, and trace around the template. Cut out the window. Repeat to trace and cut windows in the second assembled panel and both lining front/back rectangles. Baste ⅛" from the window openings on the exterior panels to hold the stabilizer in place for easier binding later.

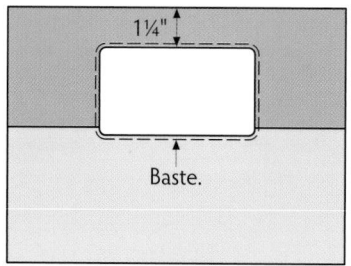

4 Layer the stabilizer base rectangle on the wrong side of the fabric base and baste ⅛" from the edges. Sew an assembled carrier panel to each long edge of the base rectangle. Press the seam allowances toward the base.

FLAPS

1 Make a template from the corner pattern on page 57. Position the template on one corner of a flap rectangle, trace the curved edge, and cut along the curve to round the corner. Round an adjacent corner at the other end of a 10½" edge; this will be the finished edge of the flap. Repeat to round two corners on the remaining flap, two flap linings, and two flap stabilizer rectangles.

2 Layer one flap on a flap lining, right sides together, and place a stabilizer rectangle on top. Sew the side and rounded edges, working slowly around the curves; leave the straight 10½" edge open. Trim the

stabilizer close to the seamline and notch the curves to reduce bulk. Turn the flap right side out and topstitch ¼" from the stitched edges. Make two.

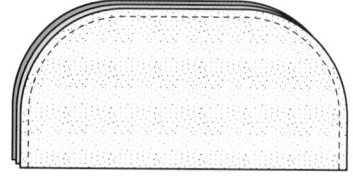 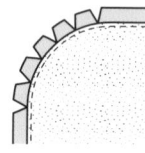

3 Separate the halves of the Velcro. Center the hook portion on the lining side of one flap, ½" from the curved edge, and edgestitch in place. Repeat to attach the loop portion on the exterior surface of the other flap.

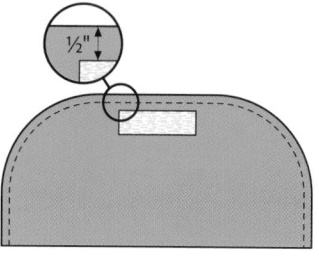

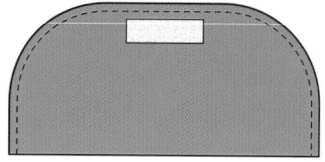

STRAPS

1 Place a strap on a strap lining, right sides together, and sew both long edges. Turn the strap right side out and press flat.

2 Center a length of webbing on the strap and edgestitch both long edges of the webbing. Make two straps.

ASSEMBLING THE EXTERIOR

1 Layer the stabilizer side panels on the wrong side of the corresponding short and long side panels and baste ⅛" from the edges. Pin the short side panel to the right edge of the bag front, beginning at the bottom corner. The short side panel will not reach the top edge of the bag. Sew the pieces together,

stitching from the intersection with the base seamline to the top of the short panel; do not stitch across the seam allowances at the base. Stitch the bag back to the opposite edge of the short side panel, again sewing from the base-seam intersection to the top of the short panel.

2 Sew the panel to the end of the base. Move the seam allowances out of the way and stitch only between the base seamlines. Press the seam allowances to one side.

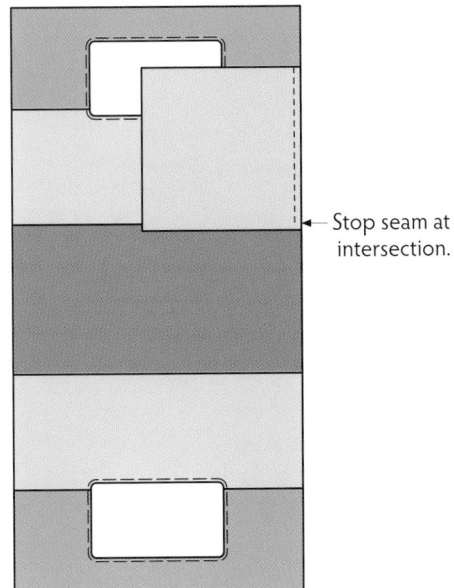

← Stop seam at intersection.

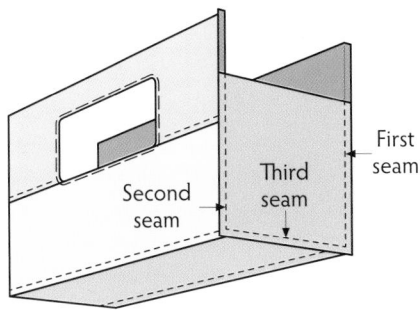

First seam

Second seam

Third seam

3 Repeat steps 1 and 2 to attach the long side panel to the other end of the bag. The long side extends all the way to the top edge of the bag.

4 Mark the top edge of the front and back panels 1½" from the side seams. Position the ends of a strap on the marks on the front panel, right sides together and raw edges matched. Baste ⅛" from the top edge to hold the strap ends in place. Repeat to baste the second strap to the back panel.

5 Fold each flap and front/back panel in half to find the center of the top edge. Lay one flap on each front and back panel with right sides together, matching the centers. The strap ends will lie between the flap and the bag. Baste ⅛" from the top of the bag.

MAKING THE LINING

1 Fold the interior pocket rectangle in half, wrong sides together, and press, creating a 6" x 5" pocket. Topstitch ¼" from the folded edge. Pin the pocket to the long side lining, matching the sides and bottom edge.

2 Sew a lining front/back panel to each long edge of the base lining. Press the seam allowances toward the base.

3 Following steps 1–3 of "Assembling the Exterior," add the short and long sides to the lining.

FINISHING THE CARRIER

1 Use the green bias strips to prepare the binding, referring to "Single-Fold Binding" on page 10.

2 Turn the carrier exterior right side out. Slip the lining, wrong side out, into the carrier so the wrong sides are together. Pin or clip the edges of the window openings together. Apply binding to each of the windows.

3 Fold the straps and flaps to the outside of the carrier. Clip or pin the upper edges of the lining and carrier together in preparation for binding. There will be many layers, so you may need to switch to a large needle (100/16) with a sharp point to stitch the binding.

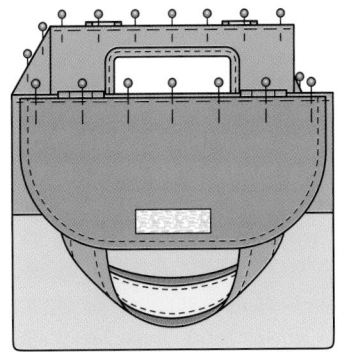

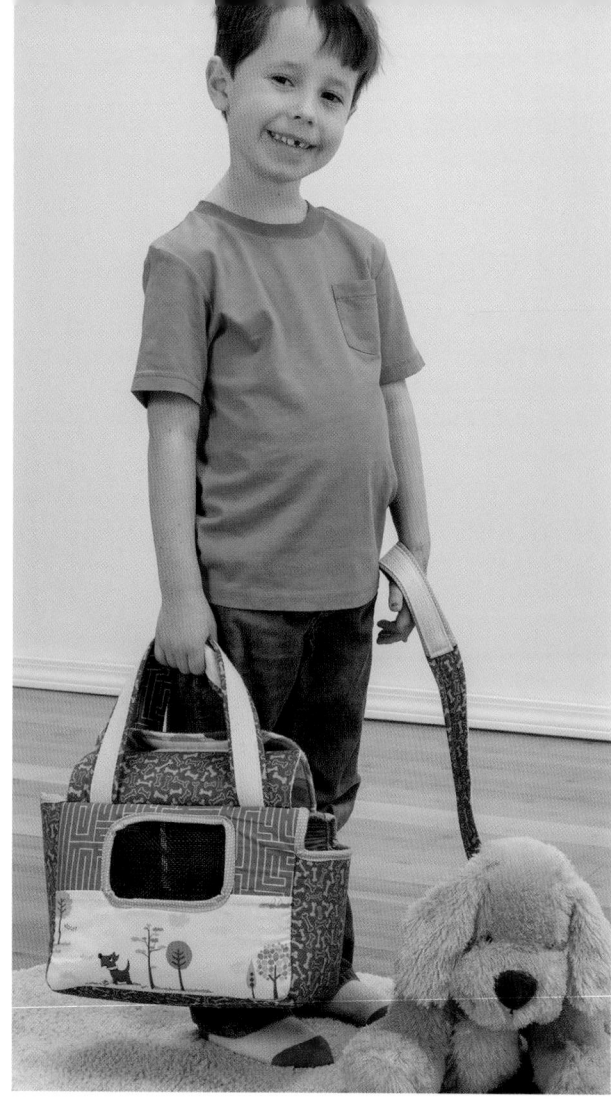

4 Apply the binding to the top of the carrier. Miter the exterior corners. When you reach the inner corners at the top of the short side panel, just ease the binding around the corner, avoiding as much fullness as possible.

5 Press the flaps and straps up, over the bound edge.

6 Trace the window template you made earlier onto a fresh piece of paper. Add ⅜" for seam allowance around all the edges. Cut two pieces from the pet screening. Lay a piece of screen on the lining side of each window opening and topstitch along the binding seam to hold the screen in place.

Window

LEASH

FINISHED SIZE: approximately 1" x 21"

MATERIALS

Yardage is based on 42"-wide fabric.

⅛ yard *each* of dark-brown print and
   green pindot for leash
⅛ yard of fusible fleece
1 yard of 1"-wide webbing
5" length of ¾"-wide Velcro

CUTTING

**From *each* of the dark-brown and green
fabrics, cut:**
1 strip, 2" x 36"

From the fusible fleece, cut:
1 strip, 2" x 35½"

MAKING THE LEASH

1 Center the fleece on the wrong side of one fabric
strip. Following the manufacturer's instructions,
fuse the fleece to the fabric. Layer the strips with right
sides together and sew both long edges. Turn the
tube right side out and press flat.

2 Press ¼" to the inside of the tube on each short
end. Center the webbing along the leash and tuck
the ends of the webbing inside the open ends of the
tube. Clip or pin the ends closed.

3 Edgestitch the webbing to the leash along both
long edges and both ends. Be sure to catch the
turned and pressed fabric and webbing edges in the
stitching at each end of the leash. You may need to
switch to a larger (100/16) sharp needle to pierce all
the layers.

4 Separate the halves of the Velcro and cut a 3"
length of the hook portion. Center the Velcro hook
on the webbing, ¼" from one end of the leash, and
edgestitch the Velcro in place.

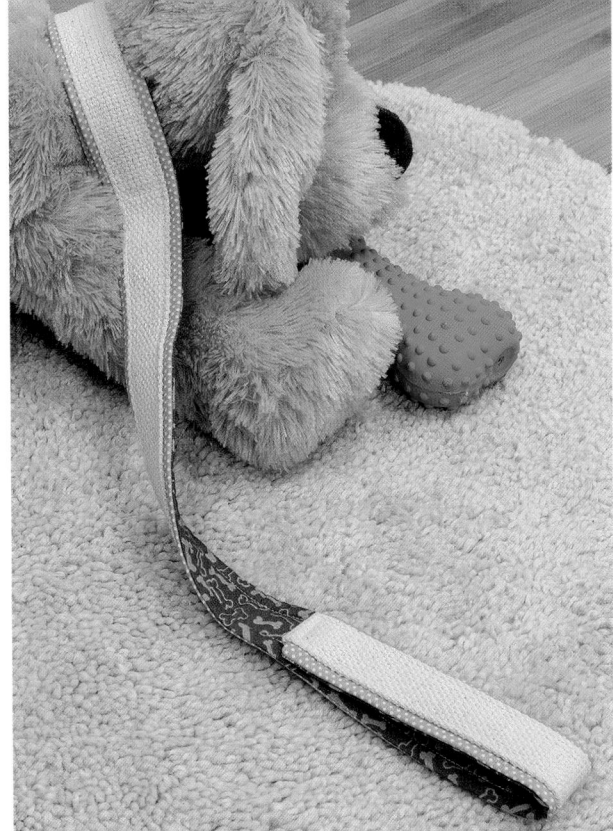

*This handy leash will prevent your furry friend from
wandering too far!*

5 Turn the leash over so that the webbing is on the
bottom. Cut a 5" length of the Velcro loop and
center it on the leash, 9" from the end with the Velcro
hook. Edgestitch the Velcro to the leash.

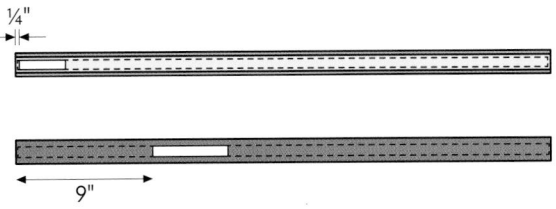

6 Fold 5" of the leash to the wrong side (the surface
without webbing) on the end without Velcro.
Edgestitch the leash end through all layers to form a
handle loop.

COZY BED

**FINISHED SIZES: PILLOW: 11½" x 11½",
Frame: 12½" x 12½" x 4"**

MATERIALS

Yardage is based on 42"-wide fabric unless otherwise noted.

1 yard of dark-brown print for pillow and frame

⅜ yard of green pindot for pillow

1½" x 24" strip of turquoise print for binding

½ yard of 58"-wide padded stabilizer (ByAnnie's Soft and Stable)

12" round pillow form

12" x 12" or larger piece of paper

Form Fitting

If you're unable to find a 12" round pillow form or you simply prefer to make your own, purchase ⅜ yard of muslin and a bag of polyester fiberfill. Cut two circles from muslin using the pattern for the pillow. Sew them with right sides together, leaving a small opening for turning. Clip the curves, turn the pillow form right side out, and stuff with the fiberfill. Slipstitch the opening by hand.

MAKE THE PATTERN

Fold the 12" square of paper in half twice to make a 6" square. Trace the pattern from page 78 onto the paper, matching the foldlines. Cut along the curve and unfold to create a 12" circle. You'll use this pattern for both the pillow and the frame.

A soft pillow nestled into a circular frame provides the perfect napping spot for a stuffed best friend.

CUTTING

From the dark-brown print, cut:

2 rectangles, 4½" x 40½", for frame

4 circles, using the prepared pattern, for pillow and frame

From the green pindot, cut:

1 circle, using the prepared pattern, for pillow

From the padded stabilizer, cut:

1 rectangle, 4½" x 40½", for frame

1 circle, using the prepared pattern, for frame

PILLOW

1 Use the turquoise strip to prepare the binding, referring to "Single-Fold Binding" on page 10.

2 Stack two of the brown-print circles. Fold the circles in half and press along the centerline. Measure 4" from one end of the centerline and draw a

perpendicular line across the circles. Cut along the line. Separate the two pieces and bind the straight edge of each.

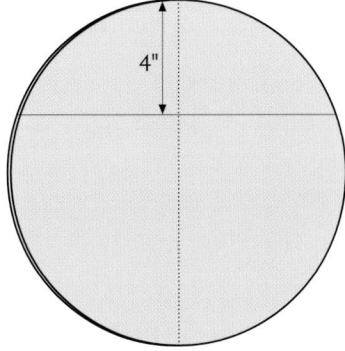

3 Place the brown pillow backs on the green pillow front with right sides together. Overlap the bound edges of the pillow backs so that the raw edges match around the circle. Stitch around the entire pillow.

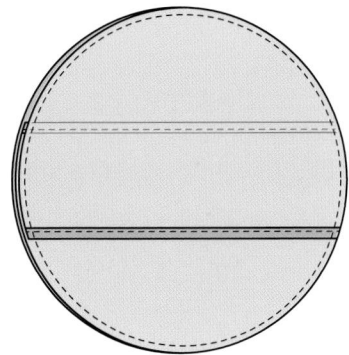

4 Clip the seam allowances and turn the pillow right side out through the bound edges. Insert the pillow form and smooth it into place.

Size Wise

Although the pillow cover will be just 11½" in diameter after the seams are sewn, a 12" pillow form will still fit, giving the pet pillow a pleasantly plump profile.

FRAME

1 Make a template from the frame pattern on page 79. Layer the 4½" x 40½" dark-brown rectangles with right sides together. Find and mark the centers of the long sides. Position the template on the strips, matching the centers and placing the template's straight edge along the upper edge of the fabric rectangles. Trace and cut along the curved edge.

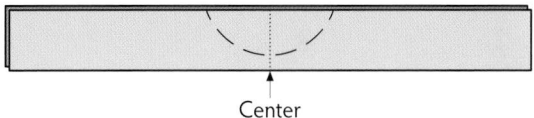

Center

2 Sew the top edge of the rectangles, stitching along the straight and curved portions of the edge. Place the stitched rectangles on the rectangle of padded stabilizer and clip or pin the layers together. Stitch again over the first seam to attach the stabilizer. Trim the stabilizer close to the stitching, cut the corner seam allowances diagonally, and clip the curves in the fabric seam allowances.

3 Open the frame layers and place the short ends with right sides together, matching the seam ends. Sew the short ends to create a tube. Trim the stabilizer close to the stitches and press the seam allowances open. Turn the frame right side out, folding it along the top edge with wrong sides together, and press. Topstitch ¼" from the top edge. Baste the raw edges together.

4 Fold the frame along the short seam and mark the center fold. Bring the center to match the seam and mark the new folds to divide the frame into quarters. Place the stabilizer circle on the wrong side of a fabric circle, matching the raw edges, and baste ⅛" from the edges. Fold the circle in half in both directions and mark to divide the edge into quarters.

5 Pin the stabilized circle to the raw edge of the frame, right sides together, matching the quarter marks. The frame is a little longer than the circle edge; distribute the extra fullness evenly and pin or clip the pieces together. Sew the frame to the base circle.

6 Mark the quarters of the remaining dark-brown circle. Pin or clip it to the assembled bed frame, right sides together, sandwiching the sides of the frame between the circles. Sew again over the first stitches, leaving an opening for turning.

7 Turn the pet bed right side out. Press the seam allowances along the gap to the wrong side and sew the opening closed by hand. Insert the pillow into the pet bed.

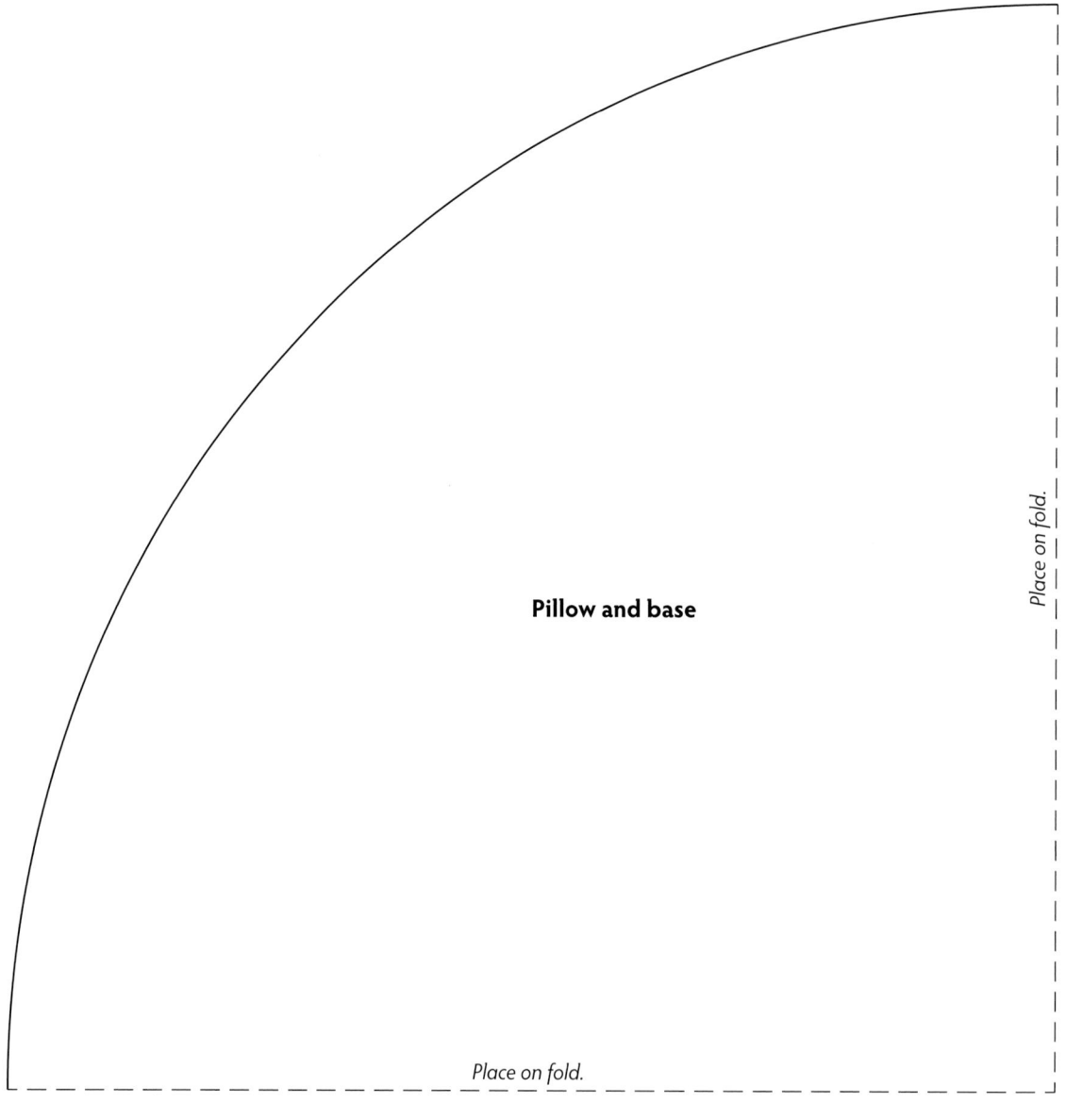

Pillow and base

Place on fold.

Place on fold.

Pet frame

Center

Guideline

Cutting line

ACKNOWLEDGMENTS

Thanks to the amazingly talented team at Riley Blake for all the wonderful inspiration and style you represent. Thank you, Jina, for giving me a chance and always being such a kind-hearted person. Thank you for the sweet packages of fabric and trims; they helped make these wonderful projects. Thank you for being an admirable company that contributes to this amazing sewing world.

Thank you to Hook and Loop for sharing such cute colored Velcro fasteners. Their Velcro is available through www.HookandLoop.com.

My sweet, sweet sewing best friends, thank you for being there for me! Katie and Crystal, you guys are amazing. I love you and love the memories we have created while sewing up a storm.

My Sew Need a Break crew, thanks for all your support. It's been a joy to share quilting with you. I'm so lucky to have you as friends, and I'm glad that quilting has provided the opportunity to spend time getting to know you all better. We've grown so close.

Tooele County Quilter's Guild, thank you for teaching me everything I know! Seriously, Crystal, Katie, and I are sometimes *too* smart, and learning that has brought me to where I am today. You're also the sweetest lunch friends.

Thanks to the wonderful Martingale team for all the amazing amount of work poured into this book. I can't believe all the talent in this publishing company. I admire you all so much. Thank you, thank you, and thank you for helping me with this dream!

ABOUT THE AUTHOR

MICHELLE JENSEN grew up in the small rural town of Clover, Utah. She graduated from college with a bachelor's degree in psychology, not sewing, and she confesses that her class load might have been much different if she'd known what she *really* wanted to be when she grew up! She eventually married her high-school sweetheart, Weston, who has always been a wonderful source of support and a great person to share life with. Michelle didn't start her sewing career until after the birth of her first child. She now has two children, Cately and Alex, who inspired this book because Michelle enjoys making items to warm their sweet little hearts. In addition to working on kid-friendly creations, Michelle designs things for the home, including table runners, wall hangings, bed quilts, adult bags, and clothing of all sorts. But that's still not enough sewing for her: she also quilts professionally with her long-arm quilting machine.

Sharing the attitude of many people who love what they do, Michelle doesn't feel like she's *working* when she's sewing and designing, because she enjoys those activities so immensely. She admits to sometimes getting a bit stuck when developing new, more challenging "outside-of-the-box" patterns or techniques. In those frustrating moments, she knows she just needs to put in some extra effort. She believes that challenging sewing projects inevitably lead to great results—unique products that make you proud, or that make someone else happy, or both! The extra effort is always worth it. Don't let a mistake or an imperfect project stop you. Keep sewing.